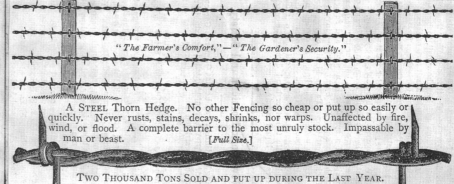

"The barn was very large. It was very old. It smelled of hay and it smelled of manure. It smelled of the perspiration of tired horses and the wonderful sweet breath of patient cows. It often had a sort of peaceful smell—as though nothing bad could happen ever again in the world."

—E. B. White, *Charlotte's Web*, 1952

THIS OLD *Barn*

A Treasury of Family Farm Memories

"The big barn would be as red as blood, with cornices of driven snow. Wouldn't it be beautiful . . ."
—O. E. Rölvaag, *Giants in the Earth*, 1927

Michael Dregni, Editor
Foreword by Roger Welsch

With stories and photographs from Eric Sloane, Bob Artley, Grant Wood, Warren Kimble, Patricia Penton Leimbach, Justin Isherwood, Currier & Ives, Sandi Wickersham, Bob Pettes, the U.S. National Trust for Historic Preservation's Barn Again! program, and more.

Voyageur Press

Edited by Michael Dregni
Designed by Maria Friedrich
Printed in Hong Kong

04 05 06 07 08 6 5 4 3 2

Library of Congress Cataloging-in-Publication Data

This old barn : a treasury of family farm memories / Michael Dregni, editor ; foreword by Roger Welsch ;
with stories and photographs from Eric Sloane ... [et al.].
    p. cm.
    ISBN 0-89658-580-8
    1. Farm life—United States. 2. Farm life—Canada. 3. Family farms—United States. 4. Family
farms—Canada. 5. Barns—United States. 6. Barns—Canada. I. Dregni, Michael, 1961-

S521.5.A2 T47 2002
630'.97—dc21

2001046946

Distributed in Canada by Raincoast Books, 9050 Shaughnessy Street,
Vancouver, B.C. V6P 6E5

Published by Voyageur Press, Inc.
123 North Second Street, P.O. Box 338,
Stillwater, MN 55082 U.S.A.
651-430-2210, fax 651-430-2211
books@voyageurpress.com
www.voyageurpress.com

Educators, fundraisers, premium and gift buyers, publicists, and marketing managers: Looking for creative products and new sales ideas? Voyageur Press books are available at special discounts when purchased in quantities, and special editions can be created to your specifications. For details contact the marketing department at 800-888-9653.

PERMISSIONS

"The Barn" from *Growing Up In The 40s* by Jerry L. Twedt. Copyright © 1994 by J. L. Twedt; copyright © 1996 by Iowa State University Press. Reprinted by permission of the author.
"The Cow Barn" from *Memories of a Former Kid* by Bob Artley. Copyright © 1978 by Bob Artley. Reprinted by permission of the author.
"Grace" from *Songs From an Inland Sea* by Sara De Luca. Copyright © 1998 by Sara De Luca. Reprinted by permission of the author.
"The Barn Builder" from *We Have All Gone Away* by Curtis Harnack. Copyright © 1981 by Curtis Harnack. Reprinted by permission of Iowa State University Press.
"I Remember Barns" from *I Rememebr America* by Eric Sloane. Copyright © 1971 by Eric Sloane. Reprinted by permission of the estate of Eric Sloane.

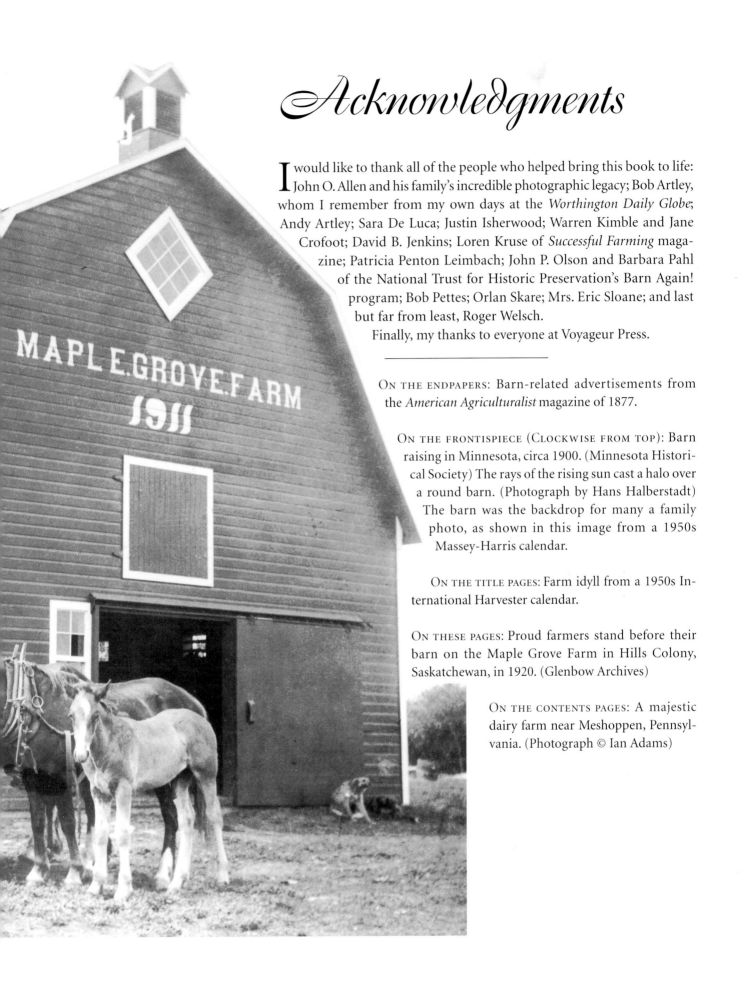

Acknowledgments

I would like to thank all of the people who helped bring this book to life: John O. Allen and his family's incredible photographic legacy; Bob Artley, whom I remember from my own days at the *Worthington Daily Globe*; Andy Artley; Sara De Luca; Justin Isherwood; Warren Kimble and Jane Crofoot; David B. Jenkins; Loren Kruse of *Successful Farming* magazine; Patricia Penton Leimbach; John P. Olson and Barbara Pahl of the National Trust for Historic Preservation's Barn Again! program; Bob Pettes; Orlan Skare; Mrs. Eric Sloane; and last but far from least, Roger Welsch.

Finally, my thanks to everyone at Voyageur Press.

ON THE ENDPAPERS: Barn-related advertisements from the *American Agriculturalist* magazine of 1877.

ON THE FRONTISPIECE (CLOCKWISE FROM TOP): Barn raising in Minnesota, circa 1900. (Minnesota Historical Society) The rays of the rising sun cast a halo over a round barn. (Photograph by Hans Halberstadt) The barn was the backdrop for many a family photo, as shown in this image from a 1950s Massey-Harris calendar.

ON THE TITLE PAGES: Farm idyll from a 1950s International Harvester calendar.

ON THESE PAGES: Proud farmers stand before their barn on the Maple Grove Farm in Hills Colony, Saskatchewan, in 1920. (Glenbow Archives)

ON THE CONTENTS PAGES: A majestic dairy farm near Meshoppen, Pennsylvania. (Photograph © Ian Adams)

Contents

Barn Blessings

By Roger Welsch

Roger Welsch appears on CBS TV's *Sunday Morning* program, spreading the word about old barns, farm living, and vintage tractors wherever the airwaves travel. His writings on vintage tractors appear regularly in *Successful Farming* magazine's "Ageless Iron" section, as well as in *Esquire*, *Smithsonian*, and *Nebraska Farmer*. In addition, he is the author of more than twenty books, including *Old Tractors Never Die*, also published by Voyageur Press.

Is there anyone so utterly deprived that he or she hasn't at sometime or another, at least once in their life, stepped into a barn and smelled the wonderful smells, admired the dusty rays of light (as pretty as if they'd filtered through stained glass), felt the gentle crunch of straw beneath the feet? If there is such a pitiful soul, we need to take up a collection to send the poor wretch to the nearest haymow to find the real meaning of life.

Okay, maybe I've put that a trifle too strong, but if you've been there in that inevitable, eternal barn, you know exactly what I'm talking about. And then there are ascending levels of the barn blessing: to play hide and seek in a barn . . . to milk a cow by hand in a barn, your face pressed into Bossie's soft, warm flank on a chilly morning . . . to sleep in a barn with new hay in the loft and livestock below . . . perhaps—oh my!—to make love in that most spiritually and philosophically evocative context of all!

Frankly, I think that the North American farmer missed a wonderful chance historically when the spaces of the barn were separated apart from those of the house. In my folklore studies and research, I often heard of the Teutonic *Einheitshaus*, an ancient farm format in which animals, storage, and human tenants were all together under the same roof. And then one deep winter in northern Germany, not far south of the Danish border, I had the chance to spend several nights in such an ancient, traditional home.

I know what you oh-so-modern readers are thinking: "Ick! Cows and sheep and horses right there in the same building?! What about the smell, and the flies, and the dirt?!" Well, there isn't any smell, flies, or dirt, that's what. If you know how to do such things right, it all works so well, you couldn't imagine any other arrangement.

What we imagine as the discomforts awaiting the human being in a barn are not inevitable. A very German uncle of mine, even with a conventional American barn, "barn-broke" his cows, as was the custom in many parts of even this county. At evening milking time, the cows made a point of relieving themselves out in the barnyard before entering their clean living quarters. A dirty barn is not the problem of the animals but of inadequate masters.

So it was in this farm home in northern Germany. A door led directly from the kitchen into the barn area of the huge building. Imagine the convenience of *that* during winter! The farmer kicked off his wooden shoes before he entered the house and the German *hausfrau*-immaculate kitchen. Only the clean smell of well-tended animals and fresh straw followed him into the house. The farmer never worried about rain or snow as he moved from his house to the barn. And the animals shared whatever warmth that migrated from the house into their area.

But the best was yet to come. That night, in a room

Respect

The barn was the headquarters of the farm, and the view from this Fillmore County, Minnesota, farmhouse front door frames the barn with due respect. (Minnesota Historical Society)

Home sweet home
A flock of white ducks congregate in front of their home in a well-used round barn. (Photograph © Jerry Irwin)

upstairs, I lay in bed listening to the gentle sounds of low whinnies and lowing from the stalls below me. I have never spent another holiday season without thinking of that most appropriate of Christmas Eve music. The sounds were a lullaby and a Christmas carol rolled into one.

Perhaps the ones who suffered most when in the New World more and more farmsteads began to erect separate structures for animals' quarters and crop storage were the farmer's family. You see, it was generally understood that one protected one's primary investments first—and that was the livestock, grain, and feed. So on farmstead after farmstead ambitious, successful, frugal, thoughtful, *modern* farmers insisted that the best building on their farm be the barn. There'll be time for a grand house later, the reasoning seemed to go, but for now, first things first.

The barn was the center of the farm, the most prominent building, the biggest and tallest, the most important, the most expensive, and therefore the most demanding technologically to build. On the North American frontier there were many homesteads where the house was still the original log house, soddie, or homestead shack, often only the quickest and easiest shelter that could be thrown up in the crush and jeopardy of frontier life.

But the barn . . . the barn was usually the product of careful thinking and planning. For this building the owner turned to the borrowed skills of neighbors and consultants in the latest notions of joining, hewing, masonry, ironwork, truss design, carpentry, and milling, and the wisdom of treasured veterans of many previous barn raisings, familiar with the time-tested traditions. No wonder that after many farm houses have fallen and decayed, the barn, if only its naked skeleton, often remains a sturdy and standing landmark.

Modern memories of barns go well beyond the building's basic utility. The family barn, after all, was not simply a structure that was visited now and then during the day. It was part and parcel of the working of the family—and the life of the family. It was customary that as families grew too large for the house, the boys and men would sleep out in the barn. The barn was the center of rural festivity—there is a reason, after all, that it is called a *barn* dance! (And if you've been

to a real barn dance, you will understand why those of us who have had that wonderful opportunity treasure the memory: dim lights, sometimes only kerosene lanterns, the wonderful smell of fresh hay, the generous expanse of a barn bay contrasting so dramatically with the cramped dimensions of the usual small-farm home. . . .)

The barn could be a place of learning too. Some of my fondest life-memories are of sitting on a one-legged milking stool listening to my Uncle Fred Kirchhefer tell me about the wild west of Wyoming, between squirts of milk going into his pail—or, with astonishing accuracy, across the barn into the waiting mouths of complaining barn kittens.

My favorite story about the barn as a learning center—in fact my whole *family*'s favorite—was my dad's, told over and over to us in explanation of his rigorous aversion to cursing. Dad said that like most of the boys in the family, he spent his time working in the barn with the cowboys on this eastern Wyoming ranch, always preferable to the physically brutal "stoop labor" of the sugar beet fields. But in this rough company Dad learned not only the tricks of harnessing horses, caring for livestock, mending fences and machinery, and nursing injuries of animals and man, he also learned the language of his much older contemporaries. He was just six or seven years old but he was already learning words his parents wouldn't even accept from the adult hired help, yet a boy, yet their own child!

One day he went a little too far in his language, even for the cowboys, and one of them pointed out to the others that if Dad's father ever heard him using that kind of language, he would surely hold them responsible for this extracurricular instruction in diction, and they would be in real trouble, maybe even being fired for their indiscretion. The other cowboys saw the fellow's logic and decided this little kid needed straightening out. They told him there'd be no more cussing. Dad, being German, of course refused, tossing in a couple of his favorite recent vocabulary acquisitions to emphasize the point.

The cowboys gathered around the kid and told him to stop the salty language right now, or else. But, being a German, he stubbornly kept right on cussing. Finally, in desperation, the leader of the reform group picked up Dad by his overall straps and hanged him by those straps from a large nail on one of the barn beams. During the day, as the men passed by the squirming miscreant, they would ask him if he was ready to stop cussing, and, being a German, he would reply with choice examples of same.

Finally, the day ended, with Dad still dangling from that nail, still German, still cussing. The dinner bell rang, and the cowboys straggled out of the barn and toward the house. And Dad could hear the dinner preparations from the kitchen and maybe even smell his mother's fresh rye bread, roast beef, gravy, and mashed potatoes. The last cowboy, the supervisor of the day's lesson, was about to exit the barn but turned one last time to ask the defiant boy if he was going to miss supper and hang there on that nail all night, or would he promise for once and for all to quit his linguistic crudity.

Well, Dad had his priorities and so gave in, finally promising never again to cuss.

And, being a German, he never did.

Eighty-some years later my Aunt Emma and Cousin Janice did something so wonderful it brings tears to my eyes just to think about it now: They went back to that barn, still standing as barns are wont to do; they extracted that nail and only a year or so before Dad died they sent it to us. As you can imagine, that humble, rusty barn nail is one of the most precious heirlooms my family has. We treasure it as if it were solid gold.

I'm betting there are thousands—tens of thousands—of rusty, old nails in tens of thousands of battered old barns on tens of thousands of farmsteads that hold within them stories like that, and with meanings just as profound to people who *know* those stories. Under "barn" my dictionary says: "A large farm building used for storing grain, hay, and other farm products, and for sheltering livestock." Somehow the compilers of that reference missed the part: "and a social center for courting a wife, celebrating the harvest, telling stories, listening to rain, and learning life's lessons."

Barn light
Many a farmer viewed the light filtering through the slats of a barn wall as being equal in beauty to the sunlight passing through a cathedral's stained-glass windows. (Photograph © Paul T. McMahon)

This Old Barn

"Barns . . . are of the land. They are built on it, and they are from it. They are reminders that all of us are of the land as well."
—Jerry Apps, *Ethnic History and Beauty of Old Barns*, 1999

Ask folk for their fondest memories of the farm and many will immediately speak nostalgically about the barn. They talk of children's games in the haymow, exploring the dark corners of the ancient building, frolicking with barn cats, and visiting the cows and workhorses. And then there was the work: early morning and late evening milking chores, cleaning out the cow manure and laying in fresh straw—chores that never seemed to come to an end.

Barns were workplaces and play areas, social centers for threshing time and cornhusking bees, dance halls and theaters—even religious sites for the Amish and other Old Order faiths. We all knew barns as an intimate part of our landscapes and lives.

There was a time when family farms and family values seemed as permanent as that great red barn—a time that sometimes now seems sadly to be gone with the wind. Changes in agricultural techniques blew through the farmstead, and in the name of modernization, something was lost. It all began when the faithful team of draft horses was traded in on one of the new-fangled, gasoline-fueled farm tractors and ended when the dairy cows were sold; specialization was the name of the future. Suddenly, that old barn—once the headquarters of the farm—was obsolete.

Many farmers could not bring themselves to bulldoze the old barn, however. It held too many memories, often including the carved signature of their own pioneer ancestors who raised it. And so the old barns still stood, weathering the winds and storms, hollow and perhaps haunted, reminders of our farming past.

Today, there is once again a great appreciation for the old barns. Many farmers are committing themselves to keeping up their barns not only as landmarks but as working buildings with new roles on the farm. The revolutionary Barn Again! program was created by the U.S. National Trust for Historic Preservation and *Successful Farming* magazine to promote restoration and new uses for barns. At the same time, similar state and county programs bolstered the effort to keep the barns standing and our farm memories alive.

Memories are what this book is all about. There are photos of old days, yesterday, and today. There are short stories, essays, and reminiscences devoted to the barn and its role on the family farm. All of the stories are nostalgic, sentimental, and sometimes humorous, and all pay homage to the barn.

The authors of the pieces collected in this anthology come from a wide range of backgrounds and a variety of farming regions in the United States and Canada. Among the authors are Eric Sloane, Patricia Penton Leimbach, Justin Isherwood, Jerry L. Twedt, Sara De Luca, Cornelius Weygandt, David B. Jenkins, Orlan Skare, and Curtis Harnack. In addition, there is an essay by Barbara Pahl, the director of the U.S. National Trust for Historic Preservation's Mountains/Plains office in Denver, Colorado, which oversees the Barn Again! program.

The photography comes from a variety of well-known photographers and archives, including Jerry Irwin, Ian Adams, Keith Baum, Richard Hamilton Smith, Willard Clay, Gary Alan Nelson, Dennis Frates, Paul Rezendes, Paul T. McMahon, David B. Jenkins, and others, including the magnificent record of American farm life found in the archives of J. C. Allen & Son.

In addition, there are paintings and other farm art from Warren Kimble, Bob Pettes, Eric Sloane, Grant Wood, Sandi Wickersham, Walter Haskell Hinton, and others. Last but not least, there are a selection of drawings by the famous artist Bob Artley, known for his syndicated *Memories of a Former Kid* series.

In the end, this book was designed to be part history of the barn, part tribute, and part just good fun. Enjoy.

Octagonal barn
This glorious eight-sided barn near Piedmont, Ohio, is one of perhaps thirty round and polygonal barns still standing in the Buckeye State. (Photograph © Ian Adams)

"Barns are counterpoints to rolling land and broad skies. They are focal points in a land of undulating hills and far reaching valleys. Many are truly works of art, each one making a special, artistic statement. Destroy an old barn and the beauty of the countryside is destroyed as well."
—Jerry Apps, *Ethnic History and Beauty of Old Barns*, 1999

Polygonal barn
A rare sixteen-sided barn stands proudly surveying a meadow near Freeport, Ohio. (Photograph © Ian Adams)

Chapter 1

Barn Lore

"A barn is the real headquarters of the farm. The dwelling-house represents the people; the barn, the work."

—Reverend Henry Ward Beecher, *Hearth and Home*, 1869

The barn was indeed the headquarters of the farm. It was the focus of all labor, and the chicken shed, pig barn, other outbuildings, and even the farmhouse itself all revolved in an orbit around the barn.

In the rush to modernization, farming experts and Agriculture Extension pundits even termed the barn the "farm's factory." But this term took away from the beauty of the barn, and few farmers ever degraded their barn with such a phrase.

The typical North American barn featured a large bay for the farm's dairy cows. The horse stalls were home to the workhorses who provided the farm's "horsepower." Above this was the haymow, a warehouse for storing the summer's hay. And connected to the barn was a silo holding silage for animal feed. Together, the barn was a beautifully compact workplace, as simple and whole as the concept of the family farm itself.

These reminiscences honor the barn and the lore that inhabited it.

"The Farm-Yard In Winter"

Left: Nathaniel Currier and James Merritt Ives became famous in the mid 1850s for their prolific printing of lithographs depicting historical and current events in the days before illustrated newspapers and magazines. To celebrate the nation's farming heritage, Currier & Ives ran a series of farm scenes that were framed or pinned up on walls in farmhouses across America. This image of "The Farm-Yard In Winter" depicts a grand old barn at the center of what represented the typical North American farm. The image was painted by G. H. Durrie and printed in 1861.

Barn-cleaning chores

Inset: Two Canadian farm youths perform their daily chore of cleaning used straw out of the family barn in 1906. It was a job that occupied every farm youngster as soon as they were old enough to hold a pitchfork or shovel. Most got so they could do it blindfolded—or at least while holding their breath. (Glenbow Archives)

THE BARN

By Jerry L. Twedt

Jerry L. Twedt was born and bred on a farm in rural Roland, Iowa. In his 1994 remembrance of things past, *Growing Up in the 40s: Rural Reminiscence,* he writes in evocative and colorful prose of his childhood days down on the farm. His reminiscence resurrects the aura of a time when farmers had one foot firmly planted in ages-old traditional values while the other foot was poised to step into the Atomic Age.

The world has now come to the dawn of the Computer Age, and much has changed in agriculture during the intervening years. Still, as Jerry writes, the golden days on the farm will forever be bred in a farm family's bones.

This excerpt from *Growing Up in the 40s* chronicles the headquarters of the farm, the barn.

The barn dominated the farm yard much as the Empire State Building once ruled over the New York skyline. Usually painted red and crowned with a gambrel roof, it was the undisputed focus of farm life. Its size and condition were an accurate barometer of a farmer's status. No other building approached its importance, certainly not the house! To the dismay of many a farm wife, the barn made the house look like a casual afterthought.

It was no accident that the barn held center stage. The financial security of the family was, by and large, contained within its walls. One area housed the milk cows; a second was devoted to young calves and feed cattle; a third held the draft horses; and on the second floor was a cavernous haymow which contained the winter feed and bedding for the animals below. No wonder then, that fear of a barn fire ranked equally with such natural disasters as drought, flood, hail, and tornadoes.

In the barn, the farmer began and ended his work day. He had no choice. For, whatever else he did or failed to do, the cows had to be milked twice a day. It made no difference if he had worked until dark in the fields, if it were a holiday, if there were a raging blizzard, if there were a birth in the family, or even if war was de-clared, those damned cows were always there, waiting to be milked.

Oh, how I hated cows! I was their prisoner. Take the Fourth of July, for instance. Next to Christmas, this was *the* holiday. The family arrived in Story City a little before noon. There we met my uncles, aunts, and cousins and had a family picnic. After stuffing myself with fried chicken, baked beans, potato salad, homemade buns, and at least two pieces of pie, I joined my cousins and other friends riding the tub on the merry-go-round, throwing firecrackers, and doing the hundred-and-one things boys used to do at Fourth of July celebrations. It was a full, fun-filled day. But, even as I played, I periodically looked over at the cow pasture next to the park and was reminded that at five o'clock the fun would end. And sure enough, just when I was enjoying myself the most, Dad would find me and say, "Come on, Jerry. It's time to go do the chores."

My reply was always the same, "Ah, gee! Can't we skip 'em just once?"

My father's answer was always the same, "No."

So with head lowered, fists clenched, and much mumbling, I followed Dad to the car. On the way home, I sulked and mentally wrote my annual "declaration of independence" from cows!

Moonrise
A full moon rises above a classic arched-roof dairy barn near Stevens Point, Wisconsin. (Photograph © Richard Hamilton Smith)

As inconvenient as the evening milking could be at times, it was not nearly as intolerable as the morning milking. Who in his right mind wants to get up at five-thirty in the morning and milk cows? Certainly, I didn't! This was especially true in winter.

A typical morning went as follows.

"Jerry, time to get up," Dad would call from the foot of the stairs. His voice seemed to come out of dense fog, and in my drowsy state, the ninety percent of me that was still asleep quickly convinced the ten percent of me that was awake that I hadn't heard a thing.

Several minutes passed. "Jerry, get up now!" My dad's voice had lost much of the friendliness that had been evident in his first call.

At this point, I would slowly stick my nose out from beneath the stacks of blankets and quilts and take a breath of the sharp air. Since the upstairs was not heated, this breath could quite literally be eye opening! My response, however, was to burrow back under the covers and curl up like a fetus.

"Jerry, are you up?" This question was asked in a stern voice. Dad was losing patience.

"I'm up." I answered in a groggy voice. It was an outright lie, and we both knew it.

I would then peek out from beneath the covers and look out into the darkness and listen to the wind howl and the snow beat against the storm windows. It was all too much! I would throw the blankets back over my head. Nobody could be so heartless as to expect a poor, skinny boy like me to get up on such a morning!

I was wrong.

After climbing two or three steps, Dad would angrily call, "Jerry, are you coming?"

"I'm coming!" I shouted back defiantly.

"Yah, so is Christmas!" was Dad's standard reply.

"I'm up!"

"Well, you'd better be! I'm not calling you again." With that, Dad would return down the steps and go into the kitchen. There was no hope. I could safely stall no longer. After slowly counting to ten, I would jump out of bed, grab my clothes and shoes, then scurry like a frightened ant down the stairs and into the living room, where I could stand shivering in front of the space heater.

Country road
A gravel country road leads back to a classic gambrel-roof red barn in Aitkin County, Minnesota. (Photograph © Gary Alan Nelson)

PIONEER BARNS

"The walls had now risen breast-high; in its half-finished condition, the structure resembled more a bulwark against some enemy than anything intended to be a human habitation. And the great heaps of cut sod, piled up in each corner, might well have been the stores of ammunition for defense of the stronghold."
    —O. E. Rölvaag, *Giants in the Earth,* 1927

Proud sod-barn owner
Many a farmstead in North America began with a house and barn made from either logs or sod. Pioneers coming west dug up the earth and stacked the "bricks" of sod to create the walls of homes and barns that often housed the family and its animals for years, if not decades. This proud North Dakota farmer poses in front of his sod barn in the 1920s. (Fred Hultstrand History in Pictures Collection, NDIRS-NDSU, Fargo)

Barn sweet barn
Framed by their sliding barn doors, two farmers survey the barnyard. (Photograph © Richard Hamilton Smith)

Once I was up, Dad's usual pleasant manner returned. He never yelled at me for making him call so many times. In fact, when the weather was miserable, he often seemed almost apologetic. My father was, and is, a gentle man. It would have required a much harder man than he to scold a sleepy, shivering boy, standing with his bare backside to a space heater.

After I gained control of my trembling body, I began to dress. This was a slow process for two reasons: First, I didn't want to go out and milk; second, each article of clothing had to be warmed on the heater before I put it on.

By the time I was completely dressed, Dad had gone to the barn. This meant I had a few extra minutes to stand in front of the heater. As the warmth from the heater drove away my shivers, a wonderful drowsy feeling came over me. My eyes closed and I slowly turned, like a roast on a spit, so as not to get too hot on one side. All the while I listened to the wind rattling the storm windows. In this euphoric state, the almost irresistible urge to curl up and go to sleep by the heater came over me. It was only the fear of my father's wrath that made me eventually draw myself away from the warmth, put on my coat, overshoes, cap and gloves, and go out into the cold Iowa morning.

I am sure the darkness made the walk from the house to the barn seem worse than it really was, but, even allowing for the psychological factor, the distance

covered could be physically brutal. The frigid air took my breath away, and after five or six steps, I was cold to the bone. I felt my nose and cheeks begin to freeze. The wind drove the snow against my face with a force that required me to walk backwards to the barn. As my fingers and toes grew numb, I looked back at the friendly, inviting lights of the house, and I swore to myself I would never own a milk cow.

I never have.

Reaching the barn on such a morning was like finding shelter in a desert sandstorm. Because of the bad weather, the animals were kept in all night, and their body heat caused the barn to be warm and fragrant. There was the smell of manure, of course. But, mixed in with it were the odors of the hay, straw, oats, leather harnesses, and the animals themselves. The sum and total of the smells was most pleasing, especially after the cold air outside. However, my joy in reaching the barn vanished when I saw the cows. They were filthy! No matter how much straw we put down for bedding, the cows always found a way of lying down in their excrement. Each cow had to be cleaned before she could be milked. This was accomplished, none too gently, with an old burlap sack and elbow grease.

Once the cow was clean, I put on the hobbles. The hobbles, two U-shaped pieces of metal, connected by a moveable chain, were mainly to prevent the cow from kicking. They also served an important secondary function. By inserting the end of the tail into the hobble, it prevented the cow from switching the milker in the face . . . something every cow I milked enjoyed immensely.

Oh, yes! Many people think cows are gentle and sweet tempered. Wrong! They are cunning, calculating, cantankerous critters! Many times I have looked up from milking to see the cow looking back at me. When this happened, I knew I was in trouble. And, sure enough! Every time she either tried to kick me or zap me in the face with her tail! Take my advice . . . never trust a cow.

We had a beast called "MAD COW." She was a big Holstein, the leader of the herd, mean as sin, and had the fastest tail in Iowa. I hated to milk her worse than

Sunset

A grand gable-roof barn stands like a cathedral above the farmyard and pastures in Rochester, Vermont. Gable roofs were the simplest of barn roof styles and often topped the earliest North American barns. Gable barns were usually built of timber-frame construction, offering less space for storage in the haymow. (Photograph © Paul Rezendes)

BARN ROOF STYLES

"In this age, art and the farm might seem far apart. Yet words like 'functional,' 'basic,' and 'traditional,' that define modern art, also describe America's farms."
    —Eric Sloane, *Our Vanishing Landscape*, 1955

Classic roofline

LEFT: A soaring Dutch gambrel roof with a hay hood crowns this classic red barn in a 1920s painting by artist Walter Haskell Hinton. Hinton painted many farm scenes that graced the covers of Deere & Company brochures and calendars and vintage farming magazines as well as outdoors journals.

Homage to Bossie
A farmhand gives an appreciative pat to Bossie before he begins the daily milking chores at the Land O'Lakes dairy in Lake Elmo, Minnesota, in 1927. (Minnesota Historical Society)

any other cow, especially after she had spent all night in the barn. I hobbled her as tightly as I could and made doubly sure her tail was secure before I sat down to milk. When everything was ready, I gingerly lowered myself onto my stool and began to milk, never knowing what to expect. I was very aware of her imprisoned tail and reacted every time she so much as shifted her weight. But, old Mad Cow was a great actress. She stood calm as can be, chewing her cud, acting as if I weren't even there. And, although I knew better, I would relax and let my mind wander. It was then that she struck! Her urine soaked tail came slashing out from beneath the hobble, and, before I could react, she zapped me across the face. Mad Cow and her tail were important factors in my decision never to be a farmer.

I must admit in all fairness, however, that milking was not all bad. Mostly, yes . . . but not all. During the summer, I did enjoy going out to the pasture in the early morning to bring in the cows. I would stuff a piece of twine in my pocket, and upon reaching the pasture, would catch one of the horses. I then made a hackamore out of the twine and rode home, driving the cows before me.

I particularly remember one morning when I was nine. The sun had just cleared the eastern horizon, and there was still a crispness to the air. It was one of those mornings when just breathing was pure enjoyment. As I reached the crest of a small hill and looked out over the pasture, I had the strange feeling that I was seeing it for the first time. The dew was heavy, and the reflected sunlight made the pasture look like a shimmering lake of silver. Even the slow moving, muddy creek that wound through the pasture was sparkling. Framing this almost fairyland picture were fields of deep green corn and ripened oats. I took a long, cold drink of water from the pasture's artisan well and looked at this scene for several minutes. I was aware of something special happening to me, but it wasn't until years later that I realized an awareness and appreciation of nature had been born that morning.

Beside bringing in the cows, I also fondly remember the milk wars. These occurred periodically throughout the summer, but only during the evening milking, and only when my brothers and I were doing the milking. Dad did not tolerate milk wars.

The battle usually commenced when my older brother, Pete, was milking the cow directly behind the one I was milking. This gave him a clear shot at my

back. And at such close range, he couldn't miss. He pointed one of the cow's port side teats at my back and hit me just above the belt line, causing the milk to run down into my pants. The war was on! I turned sideways and squirted back at him. But, he had his cow for protection, so all I could shoot at were his hands or his legs. All the while, he could rake me from top to bottom. The fight lasted as long as I could stand being squirted or until the cows got so mad at the rough handling that they began to kick.

Quite naturally when our positions were reversed, I wanted to get even and squirt Pete. Since he was five years older and promised to beat me up if I did, I was afraid to act. After each dousing, I racked my brain for a way to even the score. One day, the answer came.

I was sitting on my stool, all wet and sticky and boiling mad, when the idea was born. A lob! Use the same principle as a cannon shooting over a hill. I waited until Pete had moved to a cow three in back of me, calculated the correct angle, then let it fly. My first squirt fell a little short, but the next one was right on the money. Pete's reaction was a surprised yelp!

"Hey! You quit that!" he yelled.

"You started it!" was my reply, as I lobbed squirt after squirt down on his head.

He tried to squirt me, but there were two cows between us so he didn't even come close. All he could do was sit there and take it! Of course, being five years older, he didn't take it very long.

"Jerry, you quit it or I'll knock you in the gutter!" he roared.

"You started it!"

"I don't care! If you don't stop, you're going to get it!" Not wanting whatever he was in the mood to give, I fired one last squirt, then quit. I had finally gotten Pete wet, and I was one happy boy!

The only good thing I can say about cows is that they had calves. Calves were a lot of fun. I often thought it was a shame that a happy, fun-loving calf had to grow up to be a sour old cow or a grumpy bull.

Dad allowed the calves to suck from their mothers from four to six days before being weaned. Weaning was always a sad time because the calves would cry for their mothers, and the cows would stand outside the barn and bellow for their young. But, if Dad were going to have any cream to sell, he couldn't let the calves drink it all.

Since the calves still needed milk, we gave each a

Barn-raising contest

LEFT: Once upon a time, everyone in the area halted work on their own farms to come to the aid of a neighbor who needed a new barn built. Workers accepted no pay beyond a hearty lunch befitting the labor they had put in and the assurance that others would reciprocate when the need arose. And if a barn need building, why not make a contest of the work? These neighbors gathered to raise a barn in 1912 in Roland, Manitoba, and divided up into two teams to race in constructing their halves of the barn. (Glenbow Archives)

OLD-TIME BARN RAISINGS

"Architecturally speaking, the pioneer builder showed his ignorance gracefully. His implements
were a square, a compass, a straight-edge, and little else but good sound logic. What resulted
was a severe and simple beauty without embellishment."
  —Eric Sloane, *American Barns and Covered Bridges*, 1954

Framing the barn
LEFT: The barn-raising contest appeared to be a tie, and the full barn was framed in just sixty-five minutes. The two crews then took a well-deserved break to pose for the photographer while perched on their masterpiece. (Glenbow Archives)

Finishing touches
ABOVE: A crew of Minnesota farmers shingles the gambrel roof of a new barn near Almelund in 1913. (Minnesota Historical Society)

Hoarfrost
Hoarfrost and morning fog cover a veteran barn in LaSalle County, Illinois. (Photograph © Willard Clay)

35

"Winter Memories"
Virginia folk artist Sandi Wickersham paints from her memories of growing up on a farm. Her vividly colored works are flush with details from her rural past, including a covered bridge, a winter picnic on a star quilt, and a Mail Pouch barn. Most of her paintings also include an image of herself as a young girl with blonde pigtails and her black Labrador retriever Coalie. (Artwork © Sandi Wickersham)

A VISION OF UTOPIA:
POLYGONAL AND ROUND BARNS

"This form of building [the octagonal barn], properly understood, would lead farmers to abandon the building of a separate barn for each specific purpose, and to providing for all their necessities under one roof."
　　—Farmer Elliott W. Stewart, *National Live-Stock Journal*, 1878

Round barn

Octagonal and polygonal barns date back to George Washington's sixteen-sided barn of 1793. But it wasn't until physics professor Franklin Hiriam King of the Wisconsin Agricultural Experiment Station in Madison published plans for a true balloon-frame cylindrical barn in 1890 that the movement to build round barns boomed. Balloon-framed round barns were seen as a vast improvement over traditional rectangular barns in their efficiency: With a silo in the center, grain storage was always near to hand for feeding cattle. From 1900 through the 1920s, round barns proliferated through parts of the Midwest where forward-thinking builders and farmers took a step toward a bright new future for agriculture. This large round barn still stands in Vermilion County, Indiana. (Photograph © Ian Adams)

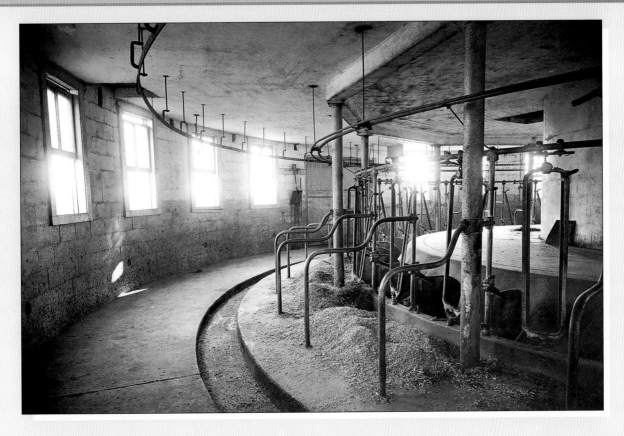

Pure efficiency

The glory of the round barn was in its efficiency, as shown in this vintage photograph of a newly built round barn in Washington, Illinois. For some religious sects, round barns held other values: They lacked inside corners for evil spirits to hide in. (Photograph © J. C. Allen and Son)

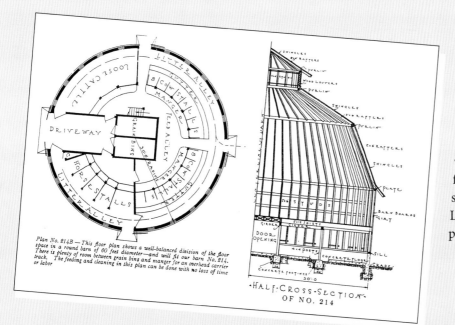

Plan No. 214B — *This floor plan shows a well-balanced division of the floor space in a round barn of 60 feet diameter—and will fit our barn No. 214. There is plenty of room between grain bins and manger for an overhead carrier track. The feeding and cleaning in this plan can be done with no loss of time or labor*

·HALF·CROSS·SECTION· OF NO. 214

Round barn plans

In the 1910s and 1920s, round barns were best built with the advanced new balloon-frame construction technique that was all the rage. This floorplan and elevation show the layout of a Louden Machinery Company barn.

measured amount in a pail. However, before we could do this, we had to teach them how to drink from a pail. This was both maddening and funny.

Dad began by backing a calf into a corner. He then straddled it, one leg on each side of the calf's neck, and pushed its head down into the pail of milk. Usually the poor calf just stood there bug-eyed and blew bubbles. There was always one or two, who struggled, bucked, and ended up knocking the pail out of Dad's hands. I remember one calf who, in attempting to break away, got the handle of the pail caught around its head. It charged around the pen, making gurgling noises and bouncing off the walls and the other calves. I thought the whole thing was hilarious, but Dad, in hot pursuit, failed to see the humor of the situation.

Somehow, the calves learned to drink. It was then they were turned over to me. My problem was just the opposite from Dad's. When they saw me coming with the pails, the calves attacked. To keep from spilling the milk and being knocked over, I did some broken field running that would do a pro half-back proud. My acrobatics didn't always work. More than once, the pails went one way, and I went the other. This situation wasn't nearly as funny as when it happened to Dad.

Even though a farmer spent the majority of his barn time with cows, his favorite area was the horse stalls. There was a quiet majesty about those huge, solid, draft horses that most farmers found hard to resist. A well matched team of pulling horses was a source of pride and envy. Many contented hours were spent grooming and caring for the great beasts.

Until 1942, when Dad bought his first tractor, our barn was overflowing with horses. He had three main work teams, plus two or three brood mares, who could be pressed into service, and a number of colts. When all were in the barn, it was an enthralling place for a little boy. I would sit in a hay bunk and watch as Dad and our hired man harnessed the teams for the day's work. All the straps, buckles, and rings were an endless source of fascination. And when the harnessing was finished, I begged to ride out to the equipment. Because of the horse's broad back and my short legs, it was like riding a walking barrel. But, I didn't care. I was king of the road!

Like all small farm boys, I was constantly pestering to drive the horses. With two of the three teams, Dick and Dave, and Max and Lady, Dad let me sit in his lap and hold onto the reins, but never when he was driving the third team, Dan and Dude. I never understood why until a late summer morning in June, 1942.

It was nearly noon on one of those hot, Iowa days that makes the corn grow. Our hired man, Orlin Britson, had been cultivating corn with a single row cultivator, pulled by Dan and Dude. I looked down the road from our front porch and saw that Orlin was coming in for dinner. I was about to run down the road and ask if I could drive the horses, when something scared Dan and Dude. In an instant their gentle trot became a dead run! Orlin yelled and pulled on the reins. The horses responded by going faster. As they turned into the farmyard, I could see the whites of their terror-filled eyes. The cultivator careened around the corner, and Orlin either jumped or fell off. He was not hurt, but his face was as white as a salt lick. Dan and Dude ended up in mother's garden. In their wake, they left the cultivator wrapped around a tree, pieces of harness all over the yard, a broken garden fence, and a wide-eyed, seven-year-old boy, who had suddenly gained a healthy respect for the power of a horse.

Approximately a year after that runaway, all the draft horses, except Max and Lady were sold. The tractor had made them superfluous. Some farmers kept draft horses around for sentimental reasons. My Uncle Leonard had horses that went years without feeling a harness. He, like many farmers, was reluctant to sell them because the only place buying pulling horses was the glue factory.

Even so, by 1948, draft horses became a luxury that most Central Iowa farmers could no longer afford. Their stalls were converted to house hogs, cattle, or chickens, and the beautiful harnesses I so admired were left to rot in some forgotten, unused corner. The passing of the draft horse was a true crossroad in agriculture. Thousands of years of cooperation between man and animal abruptly ended. Many older farmers quietly mourned. For them, much of the joy of farming was gone. As for the barn, it was never again the same. There was always something missing. The barn had lost its soul.

Twelve-sided barn
A twelve-sided barn basks in the evening sun in LaSalle County, Illinois. (Photograph © Willard Clay)

The entire second floor of a barn was an open expanse of space. Called the haymow or hayloft, its purpose was to store the winter hay and bedding for the cattle and horses. In fulfilling this function, it also provided a great play area. What could be better than mountain climbing up a twenty foot stack of hay bales, or, with blood chilling yells, attacking a fort made of bales, or playing tag and hide-n-seek on top of, around, and under the bales? Only one thing . . . jumping in the loose hay!

Until the mid-1940's, when baling became popular, hay was put in the barn loose. Great mounds of hay were loaded onto hayracks and hoisted by rope slings into the haymow. For a few days, before the hay had a chance to settle, it was soft and spongy. These were the jumping days.

One of my earliest memories is jumping in the hay with my older brother and sister. As usual, they didn't want me tagging along. But, I was determined to show them I was big enough to do anything they could. Pete and Herma scampered up the haymow ladder, and I cautiously followed. Since the barn was full of hay, I was required to climb the entire length of the nearly forty foot ladder. Being only five, I hesitated, but my desire to follow Pete and Herma was stronger than my fear, so up I went.

I didn't set any world records going up that ladder, but I did make it. Pete and Herma helped me from the ladder and dumped me into the sweet smelling hay. The aroma alone made the climb worth the effort. Nothing smells better than fresh hay. Naturally, there was much running, pushing, and falling down. But falling was fun! The haymow was like a gigantic featherbed.

Just bouncing in the hay soon became too tame for Pete, so he climbed up to the pulley platform. This was a small platform at the very top of the barn on the rear wall. From there, he grabbed onto the barn rope, which stretched from the large front door to the back wall pulley and down to the ground. He swung himself out, hand over hand, then dropped onto the hay. Since Herma and I were both too small to try it, all we could do was look on with awe and envy as Pete, time after time, repeated his jump. I promised myself that

Dairy barn in the fog
Morning fog shrouds a gambrel-roofed dairy barn in Tioga County, New York. (Photograph © Ian Adams)

one day I would jump like that. I did, of course, and the experience proved to be everything I had imagined.

As a farm boy grew, the haymow continued to hold attractions. Most every boy had a basketball hoop in the hayloft. On spring evenings, the haymow, emptied of its winter load, would reverberate with the sound of a dribbling basketball. I was never a very good player on a regular basketball court, but in my barn, I was a dead-eye terror! I regularly beat boys who were much better than myself. The reason was that, due to the barn's dimensions, my hoop was set at nine-and-a-half feet instead of the regulation ten feet. Everybody overshot!

Using corn ears to hunt pigeons at night in the haymow was also great fun. First, we broke a number of corn ears in half. Then, we took a flashlight and the corn ears and quietly climbed up into the dark haymow. It was necessary to be quiet so as not to awaken the sleeping pigeons. When a pigeon was spotted and everyone was ready, the boy with the flashlight turned it on. The pigeon froze in the light, and the boys with the corn ears let fly! Although the corn ears made a terrible racket when they hit the barn wall or roof, the pigeon was never in much danger, especially from me. I had the control of a knuckle-baller throwing into a hurricane. But, the plotting and sneaking around in the blackness of the haymow was the real fun. Nobody actually cared that we never hit the pigeons.

It would be impossible to write about the haymow without a word or two on the delicate subject of sex. Anyone who has heard a farmer's daughter or traveling salesman joke knows that the haymow was the farm's center of sin and lust. Into the haymow a young man would take his sweet, young thing, and, in the mellow darkness, he would make passionate love to her. Ah, if it were only true!

Like so many popular beliefs, the haymow as a rendezvous for young lovers has been highly exaggerated. I'm not saying that it never served that purpose, but anyone knows that a blanket spread in the silent seclusion of a corn field was much safer! There were three drawbacks to using the haymow: one, the farmer might decide to feed his animals at a most inopportune time; two, the hay was scratchy; three, the girl's hair would become entangled with hay, which was a dead give away to any eagle-eyed parent.

Nevertheless, I did listen with great rapture to all the "sex in the haymow" stories. The hormones raced through my body as I imagined myself in the situation. But, alas, imagining was as far as I got. I could never figure out how to con a girl into going up into the haymow with me. The closest I ever came to bodily contact with a girl in the haymow was fouling my sister, Herma, in a basketball game!

The barn was designed to meet the needs of the general family farm. As long as a farmer kept a few horses, a small herd of milk cows, and some feed cattle, the barn remained the center of activity. But, as general farming gave way to specialized farming, the barn went from the status of indispensable to white elephant.

The demise of the once proud barn was almost obscenely swift. It began in the '40s with the selling of the draft horses and was completed in the '50s when the milk cows were sold. Two major areas of the barn ceased to function. If the barn were in good condition, attempts were made to develop these areas for other purposes, but, in most cases the result was less than satisfactory. Farmers quickly learned that they were better off building a modern hog house or cattle shed than trying to renovate the barn. This led to barns being bulldozed or simply allowed to stand empty and rot on their foundations. There is a rueful joke among farmers that in any wind of above twenty miles per hour, anyone with an old barn puts his wind insurance policy in his pocket and pushes against the barn for all he's worth. It is a sad irony that the loss of a building, which fifty years ago would have been considered a disaster, is now thought to be a blessing.

Within another thirty years, the great, Iowa barns will exist only in the memories of old men who spent many happy childhood hours within them. The noble structures will be replaced by squat, characterless, one-story marvels of automated efficiency. Their passing will mark the final mile in the evolutionary journey from farming to agribusiness.

Ancient landmark
A stately old gable-roof barn weathers the winter snows in Cuyahoga Valley, Ohio. (Photograph © Ian Adams)

GEORGICAL

By Cornelius Weygandt

A georgical is a poem based on agricultural themes, a term derived from the Greek word for a farmer, *georgos*. Georgical is a fitting name for this reminiscence of Pennsylvania barns by Cornelius Weygandt, who was an English professor at the University of Pennsylvania and the author of numerous scholarly works.

Weygandt was proud of his own Pennsylvania Dutch heritage. The term "Dutch" was an American bastardization of the German word *Deutsch* and thus became something of a misnomer as many people to this day think of the Pennsylvania Dutch as hailing from the Netherlands when they were actually early German immigrants.

Weygandt wrote of the customs and culture of the Pennsylvania Dutch in his folksy books blending memories and history, including *A Passing America* (1932), *The Dutch Country* (1939), *The Plenty of Pennsylvania* (1942), and many more.

This excerpt comes from *The Red Hills: A Record of Good Days Outdoors and In, With Things Pennsylvania Dutch* (1929). It is a prose poem rich in imagery devoted to the Pennsylvania Dutch barns and the people who built them.

It is a worn witticism in Pennsylvania that we still vote for Andrew Jackson in Berks. This saying, interpreted with sympathy for us, means that things change so slowly in the heart of the Red Hills that people are doing there what they did in the days before the Mexican War. Interpreted without sympathy for us it means that the "Dumb Dutch" do not know that the world moves. A libel, some of us declare the last interpretation, a half libel others. There are those among us who will admit it has in it a modicum of truth, if it be taken, of course, figuratively. In any event it serves to point out that we Pennsylvania Dutch are the most conservative people in America. We still approve strongly of all Andrew Jacksons, of their works and of their ways.

There is one large exception to our conservatism. We have always been quick to accept new developments in farming, new kinds of agricultural machinery, new ways of fertilizing land, new breeds of stock, new grains and grasses and varieties of fruit. Barred rocks and silos and alfalfa became the vogue in all the "Dutch" counties as quickly as anywhere in the States.

Old ways, however, in household economy, in family government, in allegiance to church and political party, did persist among us longer than in almost any part of the country. Down to 1900 the standards and the ways of living were about what they had been for a century. We were still largely a farming people, with nearly all the old-country crafts demanded by a farming people descending from father to son among artisans who were also something of artists.

So, at the end of the nineteenth century, it could be said that the barn was the symbol of the Pennsylvania Dutch, people and countryside. The barn dominated the life of the farm as its greater proportions dominated the many other buildings, and the plantings of trees, orchard trees and shade trees both, about the homeyard. The barn generally stood well out of the dooryard, and sometimes across the road from the

Georgical
Two white horses glow in the morning sun as they stand in their pasture before a typical gambrel-roof barn in Ft. Mill, South Carolina. (Photograph © Kelly Culpepper/Transparencies, Inc.)

Stone barn

An Amish farmer plows his spring fields with a team of six workhorses in the shadow of a gable-roof stone barn. The vertical slits built into the barn walls were common on old stone barns in the days before glass windows were readily available. The slits offered both light and ventilation. This Lancaster County, Pennsylvania, barn was also crowned by a multitude of lightning rods. (Photograph © Jerry Irwin)

49

HEXOLOGY: BARN HEX SIGNS

"A belief in witchcraft lingers here and there in the dark places of the Pennsylvania countryside. The various racial elements that settled in the state brought from the Old World big ancestral cargoes of superstitions and legends, some of which persist today. These ancient beliefs exist alongside orthodox religion and have been preserved by the people as part of their living traditions."
   —Edwin Valentine Mitchell, *It's an Old Pennsylvania Custom*, 1947

Hex signs and witch windows
Hex signs were believed to bring luck and fertility to farms, ward off lightning strikes, and bewitch evil spirits. The designs were influenced by religious symbols, quilt patterns, and folk sign painters' imaginations. White trim painted around doors and windows was called "devil doors" and "witch windows," and discouraged evil spirits from entering the barn. (Photograph © Jerry Irwin)

Hex signs
A Pennsylvania Dutch old-timer feeds his chickens below the safety of the hex signs painted on his bank barn. Folklore states that hex signs were added to barns by immigrant Germans—known as "Dutch" from the German word *Deutsch*—to ward off evil influences and bring good luck. Others say they were derived from advertisements posted on barns that carried coverage from the Insurance Company of North America and the Sun Fire Office in the late 1700s. Still others claim they were simply decorative. (Photograph © Jerry Irwin)

house, than which it was from five to seven times larger. Forty feet by sixty feet was a usual size for a bank barn, forty feet by eighty feet no unusual size, and forty feet by a hundred feet of more than rare occurrence.

All the family worked, at certain seasons, in and about the barn. There were hard chores enough elsewhere for all hands. All the year round the women folk had a heavy routine of cleaning and cooking and handling of milk, and, in addition, at this season and that, other special chores in house and summer kitchen, ground cellar and smoke house, oven and garden. Their daily trips to the barn to hunt eggs or tend chicks or poults were sometimes a relief from duties about the house. It was wearing labor they did in the barn at harvest time.

The men had, too, according to the season, heavy work in fields and woodlot and limestone quarry. It was in and about the barn, however, that all this work culminated. Here, and in the offices hereabouts, all the yield of the farm was stored, and the storing, like the producing and harvesting, demanded determined and long-continued energy. It was haying, of course, that brought all the household, family and help, to united effort in the barn. In old days this turning in of the entire man power of the place was almost universal, and on the poorer hill farms, where hired help was lacking, the women folk lent a hand with father and sons, until well to the end of last century.

In most cases all, young and old, weaker and stronger, turned in with right good will. Family pride has always been strong among us. We had to submit to a patriarchal system of family control, but we knew that the place and all that in it would be left to us children. Father might take from son every cent that the son earned until he was twenty-one, if that son worked out, and as a matter of course father paid son nothing for his work at home. Father might give son spending money, or the son might have to get mother to "knock it down" for him in one way or other, but, as a rule,

when the son was twenty-one and wished to marry, father would give him a slice off the home farm to build upon and run, or help to set him up for himself on some place in the neighborhood.

If the barn was in good upkeep, and full at the right time of the year, it spoke to all the little world of the neighborhood, and to the stranger who might come within our carefully shut gates, of the prosperity of the place, our place. This was, of course, in the days when the children intended to be farmers, too, in the days before the cigar factory and clothing factory and silk mill had invaded our countryside, and when there were only the railroad and the foundry to draw away boys from the farm, and very little at all to draw away the girls.

There were a few, as might be expected, who revolted against the tyranny of the farm, as they were pleased to call it, even before the eighteen-nineties, but they were the exceptions. Now, fully half of the young folks, boys and girls alike, are gone to town or working in the local factories that have been established along the railroads which penetrate our countryside. Those who did so revolt in the old days would say that it wasn't right to be slaves to the farm, and yet they would not advocate the cutting down of the size of the place. There were farms of all acreages, of course, in our share of Pennsylvania, but the quarter section had been the basis of the country's occupation, and one-hundred-and-sixty-acre farms and eighty-acre farms were still prevalent in many sections. In others there had already occurred that cutting up of the ancestral place among the owner's sons, of which I have spoken. I have come upon places, in Lancaster County oftenest, where there were houses of all ages fairly close together on the pike, the original quarter sections having been cut into ribbon-shaped farms to accommodate the children who were willing to stay at home. It was curious that here, in a district almost solely devoted to farming, a division of land should have occurred very like that ar-

"Star" barn
The typical Sweitzer barn—also known as a Swisser or Switzer—was commonly built by German and Swiss immigrants into a bank on one side and had a cantilevered forebay on the other side. This stylish Sweitzer barn and accompanying outbuildings in Middletown, Pennsylvania, featured matching cupolas, gothic-arched windows, and a star motif. (Photograph © Keith Baum/BaumsAway)

Barn cupola
Cumulus clouds roil high above the cupola of a Minnesota barn. (Photograph © Richard Hamilton Smith)

ranged for in the laying-out of Germantown. In Germantown the properties ran back, in narrow strips, for more than a mile from Germantown Road towards the Wissahickon Creek. This arrangement brought the houses side by side on Germantown Road, ensuring that protection and that easier co-operation in community efforts and those social advantages that come from a centered population.

Upstate, most of the farm acreage would be in cultivation or in pasture, the woodlots being rather small, often not sufficing to keep the farmer in fuel and posts and rails for fencing. That being the case, we turned rather quickly to barbed wire and patent iron gates and the like.

Such dissentients from the code of the farm as there were would, in this yesterday, acknowledge the other side of the case. If there were crops that had to be housed hurriedly and under pressure lest they spoil; if there was stock that had to be fed, no matter how tired you were after a day's work in the fields; if there was constant tinkering with farm machinery of all sorts, from separator to windmill, still, after all, the barn was a great and good thing.

What a place was the barn, say, of a November night and the cold falling. The stock, fed and bedded, voice their content with gratulatory noises, as they stir placidly at the pleasant task of eating in warm quarters. It is snug here in the stables under the protection of the bank into which this lowest level of the barn has been dug. You have a sense of all that mass of hay above you in the great lofts. It is between you and the menace of winter; it will spend but slowly, and keep all the creatures in fine fettle until there is pasture again. It is, directly or indirectly, food and shelter and money in the bank.

You have just drawn from the store of oats and corn and bran that fills the bins along the threshing floor above you. There is wheat there, too, that you have not drawn. Yellow and brown feeds have poured down the shoots in hurrying streams. The barn teems everywhere

with increase, in stock, in grain, in the fruits of the earth. In the root cellars, dug into the bank from the passage at the inner end of the stables and extending out on either side of the barn bridge, are potatoes and pumpkins, carrots and turnips, mangels and sugar beets, and apples and cabbages after their several kinds. All is stored away safely against any degree of frost. Everything you need for stock and man is here, right at hand. There is a steer among the cattle, and there are hogs nearby, that will find their way into the smoke house in due time. The cows will give you milk, and cream, and butter all winter through. The pullets in so protected a yard, with barn to north and sheds to east and west, and with so much litter everywhere to scratch in, will give you eggs no matter how snow flies.

You pass out from the stable doors. You pass on out from under the overshoot of the barn. The pigeons roosting here above you waken in the light of the lantern, and coo, and move about softly, and coo, and settle again with sleepy murmurs. The little calls blend pleasantly with the noises from within the barn, with the subdued whinnying from the horse that hates you to leave him, and with the snuffing and blowing and soft trampling of the cattle. Your dog comes from somewhere in the darkness, nosing your hand. Your family are in the lighted house across the way. The children are not old enough yet to have absorbing interests away from home. You are fortunate in your help, a stout boy of twenty, who calls everything about the place "ours." Let it snow. All that matters most to you in the world is here. Let it snow until you are snowed in. What's the difference if you can't get out for paper and mail? For a week, at any rate, you can do without the world.

There are other memories of the barn to cherish than this of late November, but none more lasting. You can recall how firm an oasis the barn was when all out-of-doors seemed ready to dissolve in the spring thaws. How good, too, the barn was to get to on those May days of plowing, when storm clouds would gather in a trice, and driving rain break loose so wildly that the

Shelburne Farms dairy barn

The old dairy barn at Shelburne Farms in Vermont was built in 1891 as part of Dr. William Seward and Lila Vanderbilt Webb's model agricultural estate. By 1902, Shelburne Farms encompassed a 3,800-acre farm dedicated to demonstrating innovative agricultural practices and land use, a horse-breeding enterprise, and a grand family residence. Famed landscape architect Frederick Law Olmsted Sr. guided the layout of the farm and field; architect Robert H. Robertson designed the buildings. The estate featured numerous barns, including a monolithic main barn that boasted a five-story-high main section and a two-acre courtyard. (Photograph © Ian Adams)

"The Round Barn"
Vermont artist Warren Kimble's paintings pay tribute to North America's rural past. His style reflects grassroots American folk art, also known as primitive, naïve, or plain art as created by American immigrant pioneers and the Shakers. Kimble painted this image of a round barn on antique wood just as painters from colonial times once did. (Artwork © Warren Kimble)

MAIL-ORDER BARNS

"Build your new barn right! Fortify yourself with the same scientific certainty that marks the towering skyscraper—the great bridge—the powerful ocean liner—the certainty of standardization. Let others take a chance with the 'hit or miss,' old fashioned and wasteful methods of construction—but build your barn the 'Honor Bilt' Already Cut and Fitted way."
—Sears, Roebuck & Company mail-order barn advertisement, 1910s

Design 2562—For 20 Cows

Louden barn plans

Firms such as the Louden Machinery Company of Fairfield, Iowa, and James Manufacturing Company of Fort Atkinson, Wisconsin, became famous down on the farm for their barn equipment that was sold in glossy catalogs offering all and sundry from hay forks to milking cow stall hardware to barn blueprints such as Design 2562 "For 20 Cows." As this 1917 catalog entry promised, "The man who keeps good stock and builds good buildings to house them, is the man to succeed and build up a business that will give him an enviable reputation that will reach far beyond the county in which he lives."

Sears, Roebuck barn advertisement

Chicago monolith Sears, Roebuck & Company was truly the farm family's friend, offering everything from girdles to guitars, baby chicks to barns through its voluminous mail-order catalog—which itself then served double-duty in the outhouse. These Sears barn kits included do-it-yourself plans, doors, glass windows, and pre-cut fir, hemlock, and cypress boards that were numbered to aid easy assembly. As this ad proclaimed, "Just as the sickle has been replaced successively by the cradle, the self rake and the binder, so the old time, wasteful, not ready cut system of construction is being replaced by our modern and economical 'Honor Bilt' Already Cut buildings."

surface of even this shaly hill land would turn liquid mud by the time you finished out the furrow to the field's end and ploughed back to the roadside. You and your beasts housed, and the beasts rubbed dry, you would run up to the threshing floor to be sure the great doors were secure against the wind. They would be, of course, and resounding to the volleying of rain and recurrent bursts of hail. How loud the whole dark interior was with reverberant noises! Rain beating everywhere its ceaseless tattoo, on the old split shingles of the roof and on the long boards of the north side! Wind whistling through the hundred cracks of the boarding, and pushing so hard everywhere that the staunch old framing of oak would creak and groan and all but stir on its foundations! And the thunder! Expected, long waited for, as it was, when it came it came with the quickness and surprise of an earthquake, and seemed to shake all your little share of the world!

If, in a moment's pause in the storm, you would open the manhole in the barn door, you would see lightning stabbing down in zigzags. They were short zigzags, so low were the leaden clouds banked up, hardly higher than the fence-row cherries, now strangely white, as they climbed the sudden hill, in the illumination of all the landscape. You would sink back on the pile of bags within the little door, content to rest a spell while the storm went wild again. Were there not symbols on the barn? They would keep the lightning away. The barn had stood there a hundred years on the open hilltop, with no lightning rods and no high trees nearer than the pines before the house a hundred yards away. Six-lobed the symbols were, in weathered lead that was still strikingly white against the ironstone red of the wooden front. Six-lobed they were, within their circle of four-foot diameter, the six petals of the conventionalized tulip that is the sign manual of all good things in our folk culture. They were on the south side of the barn, and only four of them, not the miraculous seven that keep away all harm. Yet they had kept away the lightning for a hundred years, and they were, no doubt, still potent, as sure in their efficacy as anything in life may be.

There were pleasanter places than the overhead on hot hay days of June and July, but even then the threshing floor was a refuge from the sun-baked fields without. The great doors past which you drove in were open behind you and the smaller doors on the south side open before you, and there was a draught drawing through. The wind was never still on these heights. And if there was no shade about the barn save that cast by its own walls, the absence of trees gave the wind so much the better access to all quarters of the lofts, through the cracks between the boards of the sides, the slits in the stonework of the ends, the round windows above the slits in the high gable, and the great doors to the threshing floor. There were the other harvestings of wheat, of oats, of potatoes, of second-crop hay, of corn, of buckwheat, and of apples, that brought you to the barn on all sorts of days the summer through and all the fall.

How good it had been, too, in one of boyhood's moments of stolen leisure, to climb up the ladder from the threshing floor and to work your way across the hay to the little window, circular and bricklined, which looked out westward toward the Blue Mountain. You were so high you could see over the roof of the tenant house. Beyond lay the near valley, with that abrupt gap in its further hill through which ran the road to Saylorsburg. Beyond was a line of mountains, the Blue Mountains. They were, in their misty mole-grey, the perfect background to the banked masses of oaks, ruddy brown these October days, that covered so thickly the nearer hills. How soon, you would wonder, would those Bluebergers up there be plucking their geese, and the feathers, turned to snow-flakes, be whitening all the red ploughland.

There are other symbols of the Pennsylvania Dutch than the barn. We are, no more than any other stock, wholly a farming people. Yet we have stuck to the farm more faithfully than any other stock in America. That faithfulness has been due as much, I think, to our love of doing what we want to do in our own way, as to our innate love of the soil. Though the farmer may be a slave to his farm he is freer of the domination of his fellow men than any other man in modern life. Yesterday, when he spun his own flag, wove his own woolen cloth, and tanned his own leather, he was still freer. The farmer has obviously more of the necessities of life on his own place than any other man.

THE BILLBOARD BARN

By David B. Jenkins

David B. Jenkins grew up on a small farm in southern Indiana, working the land with a horse and a mule and milking a few cows. When he left the farm to go to college and make his way in the world, he planned never to return to farming. Neither did he plan to marry a city girl who thought country living sounded romantic and wonderful. But it happened, and they eventually found twenty-eight acres in McLemore's Cove in the North Georgia mountains, where they built a home, bought a beat-up old Ford tractor, erected a barn, and currently have six cows, all raising calves. Beef cattle, that is. Milking cows is still not on his agenda.

Jenkins is also a photographer and writer whose work has appeared in magazines from *Time* to *Country America*. In his book *Rock City Barns: A Passing Era* (1996), he paid tribute to the billboard barns and a vanishing icon of roadside Americana.

His interest in roadside culture dates back to the 1950s when he hitchhiked between his family's farm and college in Chattanooga, Tennessee. His primary routes were U.S. 31 and U.S. 41, hotbeds of old-time roadside Americana. In those days, he paid little attention to advertising barns because they were as common as dirt, but a growing nostalgia for passing ways of life ultimately led him to take a special interest in billboard barns and other old structures.

$\mathcal{W}$ho first painted an advertising message on a barn? No one knows for sure, but it's such a logical thing to do that it must have happened early on, probably right after barns began to be enclosed with planks over the original logs and sheet metal replaced shingle roofs. Usually located close to roads and presenting large, flat surfaces, barns were cheap and ready-made billboards, which people with something to sell could not have failed to notice. Some even advertised themselves: On the plains of central Ohio, farmers of 150 years ago put their names on the great barns they built so the world would know of their achievements.

Whoever was first, it's generally agreed that the Bloch Brothers Tobacco Company of Wheeling, West Virginia, was the first to set up an organized, large-scale barn advertising program. Bloch Brothers began painting its "Chew Mail Pouch Tobacco" slogan on barns in 1897 and continued its campaign until 1993. Hundreds of Mail Pouch barns still dot the Midwest.

The only comparable advertising campaign was waged by a tourist attraction named Rock City Gardens near Chattanooga, Tennessee. Although it involved fewer barns over a shorter span of time, the "See Rock City" program may have been even more influential. Probably the third-most-asked question by travelers through the South in the 1940s through the 1960s—after "Are we almost there yet?" and "When do we eat?"—was "What the heck is a rock city?" Driven beyond endurance by the pervasive message of the ubiquitous barns and the chorus of pleas from back seats, millions of tourists made the pilgrimage up Lookout Mountain to see for themselves what a rock city might be.

Mail Pouch barn

The sides of barns made ideal billboards along country roads in the days before interstate highways. Bloch Brothers Tobacco Company of Wheeling, West Virginia, sparked the revolutionary idea, and its "Mail Pouch barns" became roadside icons. Bloch Brothers began painting its "Chew Mail Pouch Tobacco" slogan on barns in 1897 and continued its campaign until 1993. More than 20,000 barns from Ohio and Pennsylvania, through the Midwest and as far afield as California and the Pacific Northwest were used to sell the chaw. This barn stands by a wheatfield near Bryan, Ohio. (Photograph © Ian Adams)

Barn painter Clark Byers
Clark Byers started painting barns with the "See Rock City" logo in 1936. Over the years, he lost count of how many barns he painted, such as this one in Rising Fawn, Georgia. (Photograph © David B. Jenkins)

Many others have advertised on barns over the years, some of them extensively, but Mail Pouch Tobacco and Rock City were almost certainly the largest and best-known campaigns. Ruby Falls, another tourist attraction near Chattanooga, currently maintains a number of barns in Tennessee, and Meramec Caverns, an attraction in Missouri, has barns throughout much of the Midwest and as far away as eastern Kentucky. Mammoth Cave in Kentucky also has some barn advertising. Jefferson Island Salt once advertised heavily on barns, but their signs are fading out; I've seen them only in the South.

The stories of the Mail Pouch and Rock City barns are forever linked to two men, one the first barn-advertisement painter and the other the last. Clark Byers and Harley Warrick were advertising men, for sure, but not your basic gray-flannel-suit types. It's doubtful either of them ever came within hog-calling distance of

Madison Avenue, yet this homespun duo were key players in two of the greatest outdoor advertising campaigns of all time. Their work helped define an era in American folk history.

In his thirty-year odyssey, Clark Byers, the original Rock City barn painter, traveled tens of thousands of miles in nineteen states and painted "See Rock City" on so many barns that to this day no one knows exactly how many there were. His work made an obscure tourist attraction world famous and its slogan a household phrase.

Harley Warrick, the last of the Mail Pouch painters, was even more productive than Byers. Beginning his career just days after returning from military service in World War II, he criss-crossed the Midwest for nearly fifty years, painting and repainting red, yellow, and black Mail Pouch signs on as many as 20,000 barns.

When he at last hung up his brushes, it was the end of Mail Pouch Tobacco barn painting.

Both of them started young. Says Byers, "I was just a kid in my early twenties, working as a sign painter's helper. My boss was Mr. Fred Maxwell—he was real close friends with Garnet Carter, the man who started Rock City. Well, one day about 1936, Mr. Maxwell asked me to come up on the mountain with him to meet Mr. Carter and that was the startin' of it all."

While Clark and his crew of helpers roamed the South and Midwest in their pickup truck on jaunts of two or three weeks duration, Warrick's schedule was even more demanding, "[We were] knockin' out some two, three barns a day, six days a week. For the first twenty years I worked fifty weeks a year at that pace. That's doin' about 700 barns a year, coatin' or recoatin'."

Which is not to say that Byers and his men were slackers. "There's been a time when we would do five or six a day. Three or four wasn't nothin'. I started out with one helper, then I got two helpers. Everybody had somethin' to do—we didn't miss a lick! These boys, I had 'em trained. We was hungry, and in a hurry."

Deciding which barns to paint called for good judgment—and, often, negotiating skill. Warrick recalls the typical farmers' distrust of salesmen: "Sometimes you had somebody who went on out ahead, leasing them, gettin' them ready. But not always. A farmer was suspicious of salesmen. Anybody with a big car, a suit on, a briefcase, meant banks or government, and that was like wavin' a red bandanna in front of a bull. Most salesmen didn't tell a farmer what he wanted the barn for. But if you went in like I did and started talkin' hogs, crops, and cattle, then got around to what he knew all the time you was there for, he'd sign a lease for a few bucks or just the new paint job."

In Rock City's early days, Carter and Maxwell chose the sign locations, and Byers did not always approve. "Sometimes I'd go up to the farmer's door sayin' to myself, 'Nobody home, I hope, I hope, I hope!'" But that soon changed.

"There was an ol' roof down at Tunnel Hill, Georgia, about seventy-five feet long. They hadn't ever seen it. They'd been by there, but it was settin' in behind some trees. I knew if I could cut the trees down it would knock their eyes out, so I got permission to cut the trees and paint that barn. You could see it at least three quar-

ters of a mile—that's how good it was. It was so much better than anything they had ever picked out, and they didn't even know it was there. So from then on, they just turned me loose and let me pick the sites."

As young men driving the highways of mid-twentieth-century America in search of adventure and a living, Clark, Harley, and their helpers spent their nights in boarding houses, cheap hotels, or the backs of their trucks. Life on the road was seldom dull. In Mississippi, an angry bull kept Byers and his men on a roof for hours. In Wisconsin, union men tried to keep his non-union crew from working. "We'd paint the side of a store in a little town," says Warrick, "and there would come the little old lady in the gray hat, ridin' us up one side and down the other about paintin' that nasty tobacco sign."

Byers doesn't remember if he and Warrick ever met, but it is possible that they did. There was at least one barn—on U.S. 27 in east-central Indiana—that had a "See Rock City" sign on the roof and a "Chew Mail Pouch Tobacco" sign on its side.

Life on the road became something to be savored as the years rolled by. To Warrick, it was "like comin' home when I repaint one of 'em. I do my work and go in and visit with the family and drink some coffee. Over the years you get to know the kids and watch 'em grow up." He counseled his own children to "Do something you'd be doin' anyway and get some fool to pay you for it. That's what I did."

Says Byers, "I got to where I enjoyed, y'know, takin' these trips and meetin' people out on the road. We had a lot of fun, me and my helpers. I would dread goin' out on the road so bad till I got about fifty miles away from home. Once I got about fifty miles, it was all over then. I'd work my head off to get back home. One time we were up on the Tennessee–Kentucky line and I wrote Mr. Carter a postcard: 'Out of paint and out of money, Going home to see my honey.'"

The beginning of the end of the barn as a major advertising medium came in 1968, when the Highway Beautification Act of 1966—the so-called "Ladybird Law"—took effect. Both Rock City and Mail Pouch Tobacco were forced to cut their barn painting programs to the bone. As it happened, that was also the year Clark Byers made contact with a high-voltage wire while painting

"Greetings from Rock City Gardens" postcard, 1941

Rock City barn

ABOVE: Like signs counting the distance to Wall Drug or bearing Burma Shave jingles, barns painted with ads for Rock City Gardens have become part of roadside pop culture. Opened in 1932, Frieda and Garnet Carter's roadside attraction atop Lookout Mountain in Tennessee attracted few tourists until sign painter Clark Byers began painting barns with the "See Rock City" slogan in 1936. By the 1960s, more than 900 barns across the country bore the phrase, such as one in Bryson City, North Carolina. (Photograph © David B. Jenkins)

Miracle-cure barn advertising
Tobacco and liquor makers were the typical barn-side advertisers, so it seemed only natural to promote cures for these indulgences in the same locale. Quack patent medicines such as Dr. Pierce's Pleasant Pellets shouted their promises from many a barn wall and roof. (Photograph © Jerry Irwin)

a sign near Murfreesboro, Tennessee. The shocking experience put him out of action for months, and when he recovered, he decided it was time to move on to other things.

Harley Warrick, who never planned to retire, kept on as Mail Pouch's only barn painter until 1992. As he often said, "What do you do in retirement? You do what you want to do when you want to do it. That's what I've been doin' for forty years." But even for Harley, the time came to lay down his brushes. The General Cigar Company, which by this time owned the Mail Pouch trademark, no longer wished to finance something so potentially controversial.

Harley, of course, had his own viewpoint. "If those barns could make kids chew tobacco, why don't they put a picture of Christ on 'em? Might get 'em out of their dope dens. I looked at 'em over forty years and never chewed tobacco."

But he realized that all good things must eventually come to an end. "That's the way she goes. Like the ol' buggy whip. She's gone."

Yep, "she is gone." And so is Harley, who died in November 2000 at the age of seventy-seven. His philosophy was as straightforward as his work: "My name's on the dang thing. And a man's name has got to stand for something."

Clark Byers survives, eighty-six years old at this writing. "It's been kinda crazy, but I have enjoyed my life. I'm a strange person. I do things that other people wouldn't think about doin'. It's kinda always been that way. I don't copy nobody."

Their work will remain to be enjoyed yet a while longer. But we will probably never see the likes of these men again.

BARN PAINT: LET THERE BE RED!

"The only inflexible rule of barn architecture was red—no other color would do. A barn was something like Henry Ford's description of customer options on the Model T. He would make one for you in any color you wanted so long as it was black."

> —Bill Holm, "And God Said: 'Let There Be Red,'" *Landscape of Ghosts*, 1993

Recipe for Traditional White Barn Paint
1 pound salt
10 pounds lime
1 gallon milk

Recipe for Traditional Red Barn Paint
6 pounds Venetian Red (iron oxide ground in oil)
1 pound resin
2 gallons raw linseed oil

> —From Eric Sloane's *The Cracker Barrel*, 1967

"Painting Pays"
This Montgomery Ward advertisement offered "Super Barn Paint" in one color only: bright red. White was also available for trim.

Red barns

Barns have been painted in many colors, but the image of a red barn stands out in most folks' minds as the quintessential color for barns. This valley of red barns in Vermont lives up to that idyll. Old-timers say that wood barns were painted red to simulate red brick and wealth. Folklore has it that animal blood provided the red for the paint, but in fact iron oxide—commonly known as *rust*—was used to give the tint. (Photograph © Jerry Irwin)

CHAPTER 2

At Work and Play in the Cathedral of the Cow

"A farm is a process, where everything is related, everything happening at once. It is a circle of life; and there is no logical place to begin a perfect circle. . . . There were two hundred sixty acres of cultivated fields, woods, and pasture land sprawled out along the narrow branching ridgetop. There was the cluster of buildings, dominated by the main barn with its stanchions for dairy cows, stalls for work horses."
　　　　　—Ben Logan, *The Land Remembers,* 1975

The barn was in truth a cathedral to the cow. It was designed from the first foundation stones to serve dairy cows.

The large bay on the main floor was like the central aisle and transept of a church with stalls and stanchions pointing off to the sides like individual chapels for each milk cow. Above the bay was the cavernous haymow beneath an arched roof that was so high it seemed to reach to the very stars. And the hay door let in sun filtered through the dust like the colored rays of light through a stained-glass window.

Yet just as the barn was a place of never-ending work, it was also a place for play. The haymow held a heaven of hay for young farm children to frolic in, and there were dark corners of the ancient building to explore with due reverence, barn cats to feed cream, and the cows themselves to visit.

And when the play was over, there was a return to work. First thing in the morning and the last thing at night, farmers and farm children grabbed their one-legged milking stools and knelt down to worship at the side of Bossie as she gave her milk to the farm's livelihood.

At work
LEFT: Three milkmaids bow down before Bossie and her companions for the daily milking in the cathedral of the cow. (Photograph © J. C. Allen and Son)

At play
INSET: Ma takes a photo of junior with his Hereford yearling and Pa on his Johnny Popper in front of the family barn in this painting by Walter Haskell Hinton. (Deere & Company)

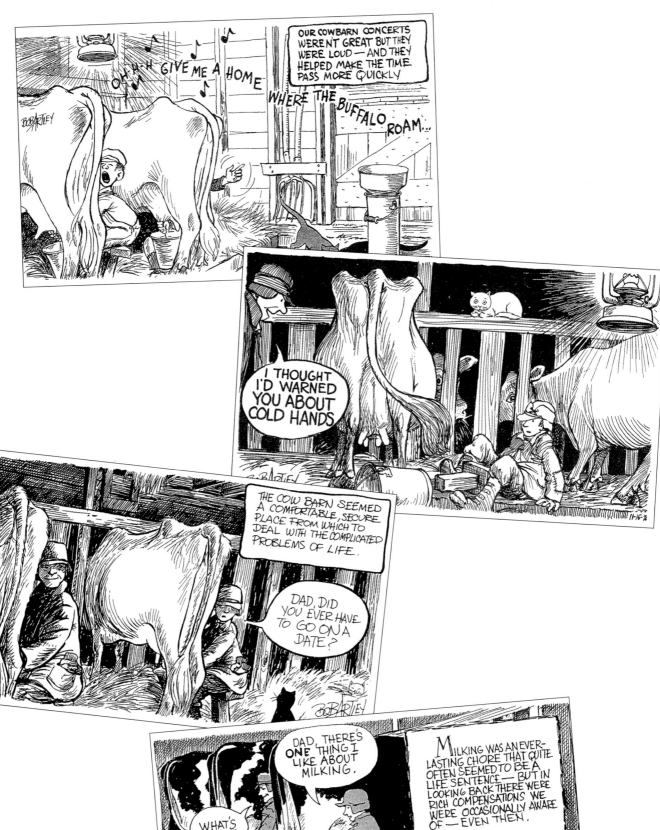

MEMORIES OF A FORMER KID: THE COW BARN

By Bob Artley

Growing up on a farm near Hampton, Iowa, the young Bob Artley not only had prowess squeezing milk from a cow's teat but bore skill in drawing with a pencil. He went on to study art formally at Grinnell College and the University of Iowa before becoming an editorial cartoonist first at the *Des Moines Tribune* and later at the *Worthington* (Minnesota) *Daily Globe* newspapers.

Artley's long-lived series of autobiographical drawings "Memories of a Former Kid" is his masterpiece. As *Daily Globe* editor and essayist Paul Gruchow wrote in the foreword to a collection of Artley's work, "At their core, they are not at all about long-ago farm life. They are about growing up, one of the half-dozen great themes of art, a theme Artley has addressed in a fresh and beautiful way. As his title suggests, he has discovered the child buried within himself, and he has dared to share that child truthfully with the rest of us. He reminds us of our own child-ness. He has put us into joyful touch with that forgotten part of ourselves."

Artley has since semi-retired back to his boyhood farm, although he continues to draw and publish books. He is also the author of *Country Christmas As Remembered by a Former Kid* (1994) and *Once Upon a Farm* (2000) among others.

This reminiscence of working in the cow barn comes from his book *Memories of a Former Kid* (1978).

When my thoughts wander back to growing up on the farm, the cow barn (likely as not) is the setting. There's a good reason for this—I spent a lot of time there.

I was nine or ten when I became fairly accomplished at extracting milk from a cow. And this was no easy task (why else was the milking machine invented?)—especially for a boy's hand.

Our cows, a motley herd, were not designed for easy milking. Very few had teats that were long and small enough to grasp easily, one in each hand. But invariably the cows that gave the most milk were the most stingy in releasing it. Those were the cows whose teats were extra large where they joined the udder and

shorter than the fist that was to grab them. My hands continually slid off those teats. When they did, they got wet with fresh milk which made them even more slippery. A tighter grip took more energy and often made the cow uncomfortable. She would fidget and try to step away from the discomfort. Many times after a long day in school or in the fields, the muscles in my hands and arms ached to near-paralysis before the milking was done at night.

To compound the general discomfort of these conditions were the wet seasons when the cows' udders were covered with mud; or flytime—when the poor critters were covered with hungry, blood-sucking flies. And fly season was worsened by the extreme heat that

Memories of a Former Kid

For several decades, artist Bob Artley has collected his reminiscences of the farming life into a syndicated cartoon series entitled "Memories of a Former Kid." These drawings recall life on the farm and the chores and many adventures that befell country youths in the barn. (Artwork © Bob Artley)

usually accompanied it. Picture, if you will, a cow barn full of hot, panting cows with flies biting, tails swishing, mud-caked udders full to the bursting point, and a tired, sweat-drenched man or boy perched on a one-legged stool between two cows while trying to get clean, white milk into the pail clamped between his knees.

In winter there wasn't the sweat, the heat or the flies. Usually there was no mud to contend with either. But a rainy, slushy period in winter wasn't uncommon and that meant both mud and cold. Winter was relatively dry since the barnyard was frozen solid. Then, I almost looked forward to milking—as a time when I could get my cold, numbed fingers warm again. I had to be careful, though. The shock of cold hands on the cow's sensitive teats might startle an otherwise gentle creature into a violent reaction.

After going about the barns with mittened hands wrapped around the steel bail of a heavy pail of water or grasping the cold handle of a pitch fork, my hands hurt and were nearly numb from the cold. It felt good to snuggle up between the great hulks of the milk cows, to slip my mittens off and put my hands up in the warm, fur-lined "pockets" between the cow's soft flank and her full udder. Even this caused the poor creature to flinch and turn and peer at me with a large soulful eye through the slots of the stanchion.

Winter was my favorite time in the cow barn. Carrying in the silage, cleaning out the gutter and spreading fresh, clean straw for the cows' bedding were satisfying tasks. After filling the cattle bunks, we carried silage into the cow barn for the milk cows at night. A portion was piled in the trough in front of the stanchion where each cow stood. Then silage was carried to the calf pen and to the bull in his special pen with its heavy timbered gate. The chores usually were done early on a winter day so that at night when it was milking time all we had to do was open the door to the waiting cows and they entered—each to find its own special place at the "table."

To this day the fragrance of a clean cow barn freshly

First light

Chores in the barn often began at first light. Many farmers defined their work day hours as "From can to can't"—as in from when they could first see in the morning light to when they could no longer see after dark. Milking had already begun at this Dodgeville, Wisconsin, farm as the sun's rays first lit the sky. (Photograph © Richard Hamilton Smith)

BARN TALK

By Justin Isherwood

I was raised in a bilingual farmhouse, meaning we spoke two languages. One being the standard English of supper table and schoolhouse, the other language being barn talk.

As children we were reminded not to cross the two linguistic patterns, not to "talk barn in the house." What was all right and efficient to say, what was manly and correct in the barn, in the haymow, or the potato shed, was not at all right in the house.

This mystified me, as even as a kid I noticed barn talk possessed a generosity of detail lacking in house talk. There were performances of nature house talk couldn't begin to convey. All manner of elementary particles, human behavior and habits was off-limits in the house, or anywhere else served by pavement and window curtains.

Any generous observation of the situation can't help but notice how this duplicity is a certain violation of First Amendment guarantees. And if Mr. Roger's Neighborhood is really the child advocate they said they are, they would instruct kids how to speak "barn" for the sake of its obvious utility. Problem was the Constitution didn't have jurisdiction on the issue. My mama did.

According to my mama, language was a matter of hygiene. What we said in the barn didn't matter to her as long as we washed it off when we came to the house. We were expected to shed language the same as we shucked our barn coats and hung them on the nails in the mudroom. Language, we learned, had residual stinks that dare not cross the threshold, stinks a person isn't aware of while working in the barn.

Any sober linguist will testify this creates artificial barriers between language groups and is culturally arrogant—besides which house English can't gauge emotion the way barn talk can. Smack a finger with a ballpeen hammer and saying "oh shucks" as ointment on the wound is not satisfactory first-aid. Science has yet to study this, Bill Moyers of PBS has snooped around mindhealing and herbs but there remains a lot more for researchers to investigate. Pain as any ploughman knows is a good deal more soluble in a crisp phrase of "barn" than anything house English can do for the wound.

And when it comes to agriculture there is a monumental list of injuries, duties, machine failures, economic transgressions that only a salient dose of barn talk can cut. Research will one day document this. CAT-scans of the brain shall demonstrate how the employment of a generous ointment of barn talk eases anxiety, reduces pain, and promotes recovery. Still, it will take more than a Nobel Laureate for Medicine to change my mama's opinion.

It is incumbent on any thinking person to wonder why a clinical breakthrough such as this was not permitted in the house. As a kid I was curious why. How come the demonstratively superior linguistic expressions of the barn were forbidden in the house?

I came eventually to understand; you see, my mama maintained the effectiveness of barn talk, the same way as doctors who don't prescribe penicillin for every ailment. If barn talk is abused . . . over-used on every scratch, bump and bruise . . . it quickly becomes useless for alleviating pain. The longer a person forestalls talking barn the better it works. There are for instance in the membership of the Liberty Corners kirk furry-chinned, desiccated widows who haven't spoken barn their entire lives and who can, if they unleash a common invective, collapse the whole dang west side of the known universe. Barn talk preserved like pickled beets, held back for the greatest need same as high heels and lipstick, hanging fire till the most deserving exponential hypercritical cataclys-

Learning how to talk barn

Barn chores—such as weaning a calf—were fertile ground for learning how to talk barn. This image of two youngsters struggling with a reluctant calf came from a 1950s International Harvester calendar.

mic moment takes on the destructive power of a thermonuclear bomb.

This was the real reason why my mama forbid barn talk in the house, to preserve it. When Moses, of Ten Commandments himself, rolled back the Red Sea, he used high quality barn talk stored up for generations so that stagnant slough had no choice but to flop on its back and let the slave children through.

When my mama talked about saving sex till marriage, I knew straight off her objective.

Made me wonder how good it all might be if I had saved sex for retirement. Same as saving barn for the choicest instance, stored up sparks like a cursory condenser, earning interest compounded every second. I never heard my mama talk barn even once. She was saving it, storing it, with the same potential as a fat cat bank account, waiting for the best chance to use it, same as Moses, who proved what is possible with the dividends of barn talk.

bedded with straw and with portions of sweet/sour silage at each cow's stanchion is one of my favorite delights. If ever the laboratories that synthesize flavors and perfumes should perfect the rich, warm odor of a clean barn at milking time, I'll order a large vial of it. Then when the modern hectic world seems to be pressing in on me too closely, I'll pop the stopper and sniff to my heart's content.

The cow barn was more than pleasant odors (and some not so pleasant) and physical discomfort and comfort. It also was the center of much of my learning about life.

During our milking sessions there were no motor or other mechanical noises to drown out and discourage conversation. Depending on the mood or on how tired we were, there sometimes were very learned discussions carried on among Dad, my brother Dean and me. (Dean was two years younger than I. Our third brother, Dan, was born a long ten years after I was.) We had the questions and Dad had the answers. If he didn't have the answer, he speculated with us. But Dad was quite knowledgeable about a good many things. Being curious by nature himself, he not only read quite widely but observed closely the world around him. Our cow barn conversations covered a wide range of topics—from the working of an internal combustion engine to the social problems of a bashful boy on his first date.

There were many times when the semi-privacy of being between the cows (and not having to look into Dad's eyes) seemed to make it easier to discuss some of the more pressing problems of a growing boy. Maybe it was the same psychology used in the old confessional booths where the father confessor was out of sight but within hearing.

There was no sudden awareness, as I recall, to the "facts of life" for me. In fact, long before I was aware of the phrase "the birds and the bees," I was quite familiar with where pigs, calves and colts came from. And in the natural progression of farm life, it wasn't long before I learned not only where they came from but how

Morning chores
Rising in the morning to do chores was tough enough on a summer day, but even more difficult in the cold of winter. The day's work was well under way at this barn in the shadow of Vermont's Mt. Mansfield as the sun began to light the peak. (Photograph © Henryk T. Kaiser/Transparencies, Inc.)

they got to where they came from. This of course took some well placed questions—during our milking sessions. And it was by deduction that I began to get the glimmer of a thought—"if this is the way animals do it . . ." So, back to the cow barn and a direct question to Dad, "Is that the way people do it, too?" His answer confirmed my suspicions and opened up a whole new world to me.

Years later, when I was raising my own sons, there were times when I greatly wished that we had a cow barn with some old, well-experienced cows to shield our eyes from one another and absorb with their large, practical bodies some of the jolting subjects with which fathers and sons have to deal.

Mostly, though, the barn was a quiet, peaceful place with the sound of the milk stream being squirted rhythmically into the tin pail—the sound changing from a "twing, twing, twang," to a "twash, twash." And when the pail was nearly full with a good head of foam, the sweet smelling milk finished with a whispered sound of "sush, sush, sush." There was the creaking of the wooden stanchions as the cows strained and leaned into them trying to reach for the final wisp of hay or bit of grain in their manger.

The barn cats, alerted by an inner clock system that animals seem to have, congregated near the cat dish and waited patiently for their portion of warm, fresh milk.

But the cow barn was not always a place of tranquillity or learned discussions. It was also a place of much activity and even violence on occasion. Because of the stanchion's ability to hold the unlucky critters, the dehorning was done in the cow barn.

Old Joab Mulkins would arrive on the scene with his grim saws, ropes and pincers, all bloodsplattered like himself. The frightened young heifers and steers (the latter which had already had a traumatic encounter with man's ideas of husbandry) were herded into the cow barn, a wholly unfamiliar place to them, and then enticed, guided or shoved into the stanchions which were then locked around their necks. In all their wide-eyed terror and frantic struggles they could not free themselves. With the addition of some restraining ropes and extra hands to pull on them, they were soon at the mercy of the barbaric dehorning saw that took the horn off right next to the scalp.

When my brother and I were small we made ourselves absent from the scene and tried to block out the bellowing of pain and fright of the poor critter being dehorned. Dad didn't like this either and usually had it done to calves when their horns were just "buttons," the removal of which was a minor operation. In later years there was an ointment available that when applied to the budding horns caused them to atrophy. Of course, this barbaric practice was justified by the fact that fully developed horns were extremely dangerous—not only to people working with the animal, but also to any other critter that might be gored by them.

Quite often calves were born in the cow barn. At best these births were not without a certain amount of violence—no birth is. When a tender, struggling creature is pushed by means of an irresistible force from the warm security of its mother's womb, through a canal that is just barely large enough and into the cold, harsh exterior world where it has to gasp and breathe on its own—that's violence! And both the new calf and the mother were somewhat fatigued by the ordeal.

If we knew the birth was imminent, we piled extra clean, fresh straw about the pregnant cow and even loosened her from the stanchion so that she would have more freedom of movement and would be free to massage the steaming new calf with her strong, rough tongue, to form an intimate connection between cow and calf. If we were around at the birth, we helped the little fellow to stand on its wobbly legs and gently guided it to its first all-important meal. Usually this didn't take too much guidance as both calf and mother knew what it was all about. They had been "programmed" through eons of experience of the species. Before long, the newborn was sucking and, with feeble butting, attempting to improve the flow of milk while the mother nervously turned from time to time, sniffing the nursing calf as if to reassure herself it was actually there and this all hadn't been a feverish dream. The quiet "moo" from deep within her throat was her way of saying "all is well."

But all births weren't easy. Too often, what started out appearing to be a normal birth, became complicated. It was very important that someone other than nature was in attendance then. Usually Dad was experienced enough that he could roll up his sleeves, bathe his arm in soapy water and between contractions reach in and turn a head in the right direction or search out

The basilica of Bossie
A Holstein cow greets the day from inside her comfortable barn. (Photograph © Jerry Irwin)

and align a wandering foreleg and then pull the calf into a successful birth. But there were times when the veterinarian would be needed. And even with his experience and training, it sometimes was not enough to save cow and calf. Then the rendering plant truck was called. Of course, this was a financial loss. But even if it weren't, it was a sad thing to lose a member of the farm and its unborn young. The bellowing of the poor cow in her agony haunted me for days.

The cow barn was also the scene of excitement. We had a black cow once that I think had it in for the whole human race. I really don't know why Dad milked her. (This was when my brother and I were too young to help milk.) I think his reason might have been somewhat akin to that of a rodeo bulldogger—she presented a challenge. He had a pair of leather straps that he fastened carefully around her rear legs right below the hocks. With these on, the cow could not lift a leg to kick as her legs were fastened together. But when Dad sat on his milk stool beside her and reached for her teats, she attempted to strike out at him anyway. Since she couldn't lift her one leg, she hopped around lifting both hind feet together. This went on for awhile until she tired. Then Dad milked her without incident. This routine occurred at each milking, and apparently she gave a fair amount of milk to make the ordeal worthwhile.

But one night the work in the fields was late, supper was late and the milking was even later. Dean and I had already gone to bed when suddenly there was a great commotion coming from the cow barn. We could hear Dad's voice, then a "whack, whack," and a cow bellow. Fascinated, we went to the window to see what was taking place. We saw the light from the open cow barn door, but nothing inside. Suddenly Mom appeared out of the darkness in the light of the open door. We could hear her voice and then Dad said something. Finally, Mom turned rather stiffly and came back to the house. After that things quieted down and we became sleepy.

It wasn't until years later that we heard the full story—much to our amusement. It seems that the mean black cow had behaved as expected when Dad sat down to milk her. But the straps were getting old and finally had had too much strain put on them. They broke and

A buss from Bossie
A happy cow gives a farmer a "kiss." (Minnesota State Fair archives)

BARN CATS

"Barn cats are a breed apart, animals that those who love ordinary cats could never understand. They come in all colors and sizes, ranging from black to white and nearly every color in between. On the home farm, we had between a half-dozen and fifteen cats—sometimes more. They lived in the barn and were never allowed in the house. They had but one purpose, controlling mice and other unwanted critters in and around the farm buildings. Most of the time they didn't have names. We merely referred to them by some physical characteristic—yellow cat, broken ear, limpy, spot, black nose."
    —Jerry Apps, *When Chores Were Done*, 1999

Ruler of all it sees
A gray tiger surveys its domain in the dairy barn. (Photograph © Jerry Irwin)

Tiger
ABOVE: A playful gray tiger lolls on a haybale. (Photograph © Jerry Irwin)

Milking time
LEFT: All barn cats worthy of the name could catch a spray of milk straight from Bossie's udder. (Glenbow Archives)

Rich in egg money
Ma and Rover return to the barnyard after gathering up the day's eggs from the hen brood at the Langgaard farm in Hamlin, Iowa. (Photograph © Richard Hamilton Smith)

suddenly that lethal hind leg was thrust out in full force, struck Dad and knocked him and a nearly full pail of milk into an unclean gutter. Dad was really a gentle man, quite slow to anger. But this was the final assault of a day that hadn't gone well. An old broom was leaning against the barn wall. When Mom appeared at the barn door she found Dad applying the splintering broom handle to the back of that perverse critter in no gentle manner. She asked him to stop chastising the cow and Dad suggested that Mom go back and tend to things in the house and he'd tend to things in the barn.

That was the end of that cow's dairy career. She was transferred to the feed lot and became a nice fat beef type. Eventually she left the farm and was never heard of again.

Our milk cows all had names—none of them fancy—but usually quite descriptive and with meaning. There were times, of course, when their names would be changed—added to, so to speak, to fit the occasion. There was Jimima, who got her name from the fact that she was an orphan and grew up in a horse stall next to Old Jim, and seemed to have a strong at-

tachment to him. We said she must have thought "Jim my ma." There was Stub, who had lost her tail to a beef-eating pig when she was a newborn calf and was rescued just in time. There was Blacky, Browny, and Hardy—she was hard to milk, and White Bell had a white belly and Stupid was just that.

When more cows were milked, especially after the calving season in the spring, the milking chore became more of a burden. After the grass was in good shape in the creek pasture, the cattle were turned out of the muddy barnyard where they'd been confined all winter. This meant an extra chore was added. We had to go after the milk cows every evening and take them back to pasture each morning after the milking. This was a chore I usually enjoyed—especially when the weather was nice. It gave me time to dream, to observe the continuous display of nature around us, explore a bit of our slough pasture or, in season, take a quick dip in the creek. The cows usually were placid animals not much interested in hurrying, which fit my nature—unless our family was planning to go away for the evening. In that case the slow pace of the cows

The Big Birdhouse

"Great Grand Da's barn is going on a hundred years old and in its tenure seen a million swallows, ten million sparrows, three point seven million starlings and thirty-five million pigeons, not counting the squab as went for supper. . . . A hundred years and still standing, one hundred and forty by forty-eight, the biggest gosh darn birdhouse in the world."
—Justin Isherwood, "The World's Biggest Birdhouse," *Book of Plough*, 1996

Owl
A great horned owl casts its wise gaze down upon all who would enter its domain. (Photograph © Jerry Irwin)

was an aggravation and I'd resort to tail-twisting, stick-prodding and various verbal encouragements to increase their speed.

We got our first radio (battery-operated) in the late twenties. It was quite an event in our otherwise insular life. The popular songs were much on our mind and many of our milking sessions were a sort of concert with Dad joining in as we'd sing or whistle "Springtime in the Rockies," "Happy Days are Here Again," "Tiptoe Through the Tulips" and several other current tunes of the time.

It wasn't until years later, after electricity had come to the farm, that an old radio found its place among the dusty cobwebs on a makeshift shelf in the cow barn. Someone had said that cows gave more milk with music. This was a concession to progress. I still think our do-it-yourself music was better—at least it was more fun.

And speaking of progress, after the boys had grown to men and the man had grown older, there came the great day when a milking machine was installed in the old cow barn. Long before that, the old kerosene lantern had been replaced by electric lights. There was a minimum of physical change to the old cow barn, but the atmosphere was changed quite drastically. For one thing there was the machine noise—the compressor that made the suction that mechanically stroked the teats and sucked the milk into the attached sealed pails. This was a much cleaner and easier way of getting milk from a cow. And it is said cows give more milk from the uniform, rhythmic tugging of the machine over the variations of the human touch. But something was gone from the old cow barn that never returned. I guess maybe it was that human touch—that man-animal relationship that has more and more gone out of farming.

87

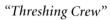
"Threshing Crew"

The barnyard was the center of the farm and all chores orbited around it. For threshing day, this crew set up the separator and steam engine close by the barn so the silage could be easily moved into the silo. Modern-day folk artist Bob Pettes paints his images of early farm life based on his memories of his childhood summers on a Minnesota farm. (Artwork © Bob Pettes)

Barns for All Seasons and All Reasons

By Orlan Skare

Orlan Skare was raised on a farm near Bagley, Minnesota, in the 1930s, earning his love for barns, cows, and tractors firsthand. He went on to serve as a traveling salesman for International Harvester for six years. He then worked at Jostens before becoming a professor of marketing and sales at the Willmar, Minnesota, technical college.

After he retired, Skare began putting down on paper recollections of his farming youth as a way to pass them on to his children and future generations. He has written of myriad memories, from the pain and suffering imposed by old-fashioned cast-iron tractor seats to the window that was opened to the world when radio arrived on the farm. His essays have appeared in Willmar's *West Central Tribune.*

Skare composed this collection of recollections in honor of the barn.

*O*nce proud red barn, no longer in use
　Your roof, broken hinges in need of repair
If you could be granted the true gift of speech
What wonderful memories you'd be able to share

As the number of farms continues to decrease, we're losing one of our most famous rural images. What can better convey a pastoral scene than a red barn, with some livestock and perhaps a tractor parked nearby. Brush in a friendly farm dog and you have a picture to re-awaken fond rural memories.

Barns come in all shapes and sizes. Most have haylofts overhead to store at least part of the winter's forage. Many have a large overhead door to permit a slingload of hay to be lifted by rope into the hayloft.

Barn roofs themselves have many variations. New England barns generally have gable roofs, while Midwest barns tend to have gambrel or rounded roofs that allow more hay storage for the square footage involved. Many have ornate cupolas for ventilation and as a mount for a weather vane.

The barn on our farm (which is no longer in the family) had a gambrel roof. It was built by a Swedish immigrant carpenter, working alone except for the few hours that my father could spare from his farm work. This interesting individual, trained in his crafts in his native Sweden, also made and played violins.

As a young child I watched him, fascinated as he meticulously cut large timbers and two-by-six planks with a hand saw. I'm sure the pleasure was not reciprocated as this six-year-old plied him with childish questions. However, the barn still stands, with straight sightlines as a testament to his Old World skills.

After these many years I still recall the delightful sight of young calves frisking, with tails in the air in the calf pen, and the feel of barn cats, suddenly great pals, rubbing against my pant legs to encourage me to pour some warm milk into their shallow pan.

The hayloft provided many recreation opportunities for farm youth. In the spring we would play basketball on the wood floor until the first hay crop was

Storm clouds
Dark clouds roil above a barn in Monroe, Oregon, as the afternoon sun casts a diminished light over the field and a sole wild petunia. (Photograph © Dennis Frates)

brought in. Past year's hay dust rose from between the boards as we dribbled across the floor. As the dust adhered itself to our perspiring bodies we were soon visible only by the whites of our eyes.

Sometimes a game might turn into a roughhouse exercise. Once when relatives were visiting, we turned from shooting baskets to a game of tag. We chased cousin Ernest, who in a moment of youthful exuberance, jumped out the small open back door—landing knee deep in the manure pile a full story below. Actually he was fortunate, not having landed on a surprised cow, or worse, an angry bull.

Once hay was loaded into the hayloft it could still be used to play hide-n-seek and similar games. Properly dried hay has a very pleasant odor, not unlike that of dried flowers. It's been hinted by others that this pleasant fragrance, combined with the comforting sound of rain on the roof, might have encouraged youthful romantic interludes on rainy summer afternoons.

Some of the most rare and unusual barns were round, for reasons that bear examination. Because they had no flat sides, round barns were considered to be more resistant to high winds and tornadoes. By locating the silo in the exact center, silage could be distributed to the cattle more easily. From an aesthetic standpoint, the round shape presented the same symmetrical outline no matter which direction a viewer might approach from. And a bit of superstition was sometimes involved

Red barn in white snow
The winter sun shines its warmth on an ancient gable-roof barn in Columbia, New Hampshire. As was common with many, this barn has several additions built onto it, offering more work and storage space as the farm grew. (Photograph © Paul Rezendes)

TOBACCO BARNS

"Few may reminisce about the hard work that producing a crop of tobacco demands: the drudgery of cutting tobacco on a hot August day; the heavy labor and danger of lifting sixty-pound tobacco sticks tier above tier, to be hung under the roof thirty-five feet above the floor; the long hours of stripping and grading; the uncertainty over whether the auction price will cover expenses; or the agonizing sorrow brought by the hailstorm that takes a neighbor's crop yet spares others. Yet, to look at the barn is to be reminded of the fun and camaraderie of family and neighbors helping in the planting and harvest, to remember those tremendous twice-a-day country meals that the farmer's wife served to the work crew, and to recall the evening's hot shower to scrub off the tobacco gum before grabbing a clean shirt and a beer."

—Karl Raitz, "Tobacco Barns and Sheds" in *Barns of the Midwest*, 1995

Hanging racks of tobacco
A North Carolina farmer hangs racks of tobacco leaves to dry in the warm air of his tobacco barn. (Photograph © Richard Hamilton Smith)

95

"Haying Scene"
Farmhands fill a barn's loft with hay while the farm children look on in this impressionistic 1935 oil painting by Minnesota artist Dewey Albinson. (Minnesota Historical Society)

in the choice of the round configuration, a belief that the absence of inside corners made it more difficult for evil spirits to hide.

Maybe too there might have been deference to a cow's psyche. By standing in a closed circle rather than the straight line of a traditional barn, no bovine would have to be relegated to a distant end-of-the-line stall. And if we can accept the possibility of cow conversation or bovine braggadocio this might be made easier by the circular arrangement.

It's been speculated that a round barn (with no corners to trap the pursued) might be the logical choice of a farmer with an especially attractive daughter. But it's also possible that a farmer with many eager daughters might choose the round barn configuration for the protection of his hired man.

Yes, it can be said that barns provided protection, comforts, and pleasures for both animals and humans. Yet the barn is another of the passing rural institutions that begs preservation, if by no other means than by picture, narration, and verse.

The pulsating rhythm of the milking machine
The rattle of stanchion as cows stretch for hay
Barn cats lapping at a pan of warm milk
Simple sounds of a rural yesterday

LIGHTNING RODS

"There is no doubt that many buildings have been saved from destruction by means of properly installed lightning rods, and it is plain that they are not difficult nor expensive to install."
—Isaac Phillips Roberts, *The Farmstead: The Making of the Rural Home and the Lay-Out of the Farm*, 1900

A crown of lightning rods
Five lightning conductors crown the ridge of a gambrel-roof barn with a weather vane lending a helping hand to indicate which way the prevailing wind and storm might be coming from. (Photograph © Richard Hamilton Smith)

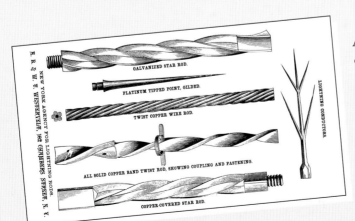

Safety from electricity
A large selection of lightning conductors were available with different shapes and design catering to your personal superstitions.

Shaker round stone barn
The United Society of Shaking Quakers, or Shakers as they were commonly known, strove for ideals of simplicity and efficiency, and this famous round stone dairy barn at the Hancock Shaker village in Pittsfield, Massachusetts, exemplified their vision. After the settlement's largest dairy barn burned in 1825, Elders William Deming and Daniel Goodrich conceived of this radical round barn—years before polygonal and round barns were in vogue. Completed in 1826, the huge barn was almost ninety feet in diameter and housed fifty-two cows. (Photograph © Ian Adams)

HAYMOW BASKETBALL

By Justin Isherwood

Justin Isherwood is a potato farmer and writer, a combination of talents as rare as it is profound. Farming has been the Isherwood family's livelihood for six generations, with three generations tilling the soil and tapping maple trees in north-central Wisconsin.

Isherwood's writings on farm life blend his sense of humor with a keen eye for observing human nature. He has penned essays on farmers' addiction for sheds, an ode to overalls, a treatise on farm dogs, and an examination of what he believes was divine intervention in the invention of the first pickup truck.

His commentary has appeared in *Audubon, Harrowsmith, Country Life*, and the *Wall Street Journal* as well as on National Public Radio. His short pieces were collected into *Book of Plough: Essays on the Virtue of Farm, Family & the Rural Life*. His 1988 novel *The Farm West of Mars* won the Wisconsin Idea Foundation literature award.

This essay pays homage to a sport that may never boast its own hall of fame or be ruined by multi-million-dollar stars, barn basketball.

*W*hat passes for basketball in the village and what is the dribble in rural parts are two different sports. As a farmkid I was amazed to learn city kids played baseball at night, under lights so bright they yield a suntan. Where's the sport? Where the zeal, the mystery, the panache if contestants can actually see the ball? The reason big league teams required the services of Bob Feller and Warren Spahn was on account they played baseball under so much illumination. Leave baseball to twilight and gloaming and even girls can pitch overhand hardball, with an ERA equal to the Reverend Mister Spahn.

Same insult was true for basketball. Played on a hard maple floor at seventy degrees, a ceiling full of arc lights and the result quickly eliminates any kid less than six foot nine.

Haymow basketball weren't so bigoted.

Haymow basketball season didn't start until December when we had fed off two thousand bales give or take from the east mow of the barn, freeing the space around a hoop and backboard nailed to the barn's end wall. As with most barns, the floor was a motley collection of assorted lumber nailed together only so succinct as most of the hay didn't fall through. Years of accumulated whitewash on the underside sealed the business and the result looked pretty high quality until haymow basketball came along.

Soon as we had the evening chores done, me and my brother lit out for the haymow. The sound of haymow basketball was like no other save maybe mounted cavalry, our galumping back and forth still wearing barn shoes and rubbers, knocking loose great flakes of whitewash. Chafe drizzled through the new cracks in the ceiling and the progress of the game amply described by enervated puffs of dust as followed the dribble.

The biggest difference between uptown basketball and the haymow kind is city folk played in the nude. Five guys tearing up and down the court wearing nothing but an undershirt and drawers wouldna survived the haymow. Our uniform consisted of blue jeans, bib overalls, sweatshirt, flannel shirt, parka, stocking cap

Haymow basketball
Basketball in the haymow included some rules and equipment that was not NBA-approved, such as this "basket" made from a galvanized washtub and section of heating vent on the Kluenker farm in Manitowoc, Wisconsin. (Photograph © Richard Hamilton Smith)

Rest time
Leaning on his pitchfork, a farmer takes a well-earned break from tossing hay in the haymow. (Photograph © Richard Hamilton Smith)

and gloves. Sometimes it got warm enough to take off the gloves. The slam-dunk wasn't part of our game, with eight buckle galoshes, high top work shoes, and two pairs of socks attached we rarely cleared the floor. The single light bulb on the west end of the barn to illuminate this contest didn't favor thirty foot shots or high scoring anything. What was fabulous was our noise, a frozen basketball in the acoustic hollow of a frozen gambrel barn; wasn't Elvis who invented rock and roll, was haymow basketball.

Illumination came from a 40 watt incandescent a hundred foot overhead, it also doubled as the heat source. The dribble was a different business in the haymow 'cause you had to play the boards . . . not the backboards, the floor boards. Some were wider than others and better nailed, as a result there were good lanes and those less good. Hitting the joint spilled a dribble. Same if you didn't adjust for the difference in dribble between an oak board and the lackadaisical bounce as comes off of popple. An elm board warped a dribble pretty bad but ash was nice. A farmkid at

haymow basketball got to know carpentry in a way that urban sports programs don't ordinarily acknowledge.

The most interesting thing about haymow basketball was the air quality. During the first quarter the atmosphere was passable but every subsequent bounce and galosh-shod breakaway liberated a layer of fossil pollens deposited in the barn beams over the previous hundred summers. By the third quarter a gray mirk enveloped the haymow and instead of breathing we just bit off a chunk and chewed.

Neither the NBA nor the NCAA would recognize the improvement to this sport the result of chilling the ball to three degrees above zero. All those high-priced moves as are the benefit of an eighty degree bounce are no longer a factor at three degrees Fahrenheit, and Michael Jordan is no longer on the Wheaties box. Air Jordan is the result of an over-heated ball, more akin to a hotair balloon and anybody willing to hang on.

In the haymow version the basketball bounces with reluctance. To get the same effect in a gymnasium you'd have to half fill the ball with water and freeze it. What

GRACE

By Sara De Luca

Sara De Luca writes in her memoir
Dancing the Cows Home: A Wisconsin
Girlhood *(1996) of the hardships of*
farming as well as the joys, of the struggles
as well as the triumphs. Her collection of
poems, Songs From an Inland Sea *(1998),*
continues her farm saga.

This poem tells of playing in that
heaven of hay, the barn loft, and the grace
that surrounded one child's ecapades.

Grim duty took me to the barn
each night at choring time.
I trailed behind my father whose reluctant gait
was joyless as my own.

My little sister—only five—
relished that humid, heaving place.
A chord of perfume—briny mix of cow
       manure,

raw milk, corn silage, moldy hay and steaming
       piss—
drew her inside.

There she amused herself with risky games—
cat chasing, rope swinging, hay-hole diving,
to name just a few. One night she threw herself
into a nest of broken bales and came up
marked by bloody stripes on either side
of her small neck.

Look, Daddy! Here's that old pitchfork you lost!
I landed right between the tines!
He didn't hear at first, good ear and forehead
pressed into his work. She called again—
Look, Daddy!
Perfect landing!

He left milkers surging on empty udders
and rocked his saved child there in the hay,
back and forth, back and forth.
And when I glimpsed his face in that dim
       manger;
it looked strangely bright, washed bare
by gratitude and grace.

we played with wasn't a basketball as much as orange cement. It didn't bounce, it compressed atomic nuclei. If it wasn't for the intrinsic elasticity in the barn boards there wouldn't have been a game. A well-engaged contest allied the barn into the game plan, and the floor itself warped as we tumbled back and forth. We could feel the barn's oscillation and tried to bring our game in unison with it, good training for those who might one day be ploughmen.

When city cousins visited they sneered at our "court" and offered to play us with one arm tied behind their back.

"You call this a basketball court?" they said haughtily.

"Surely brethren, we do."

"Well then, let's make it interesting."

"Such as . . ." said we.

"How about five dollars; you guys got five dollars?" We nodded.

They, you see, had never played with gloves on and the floor boards all looked the same and the light there was less than what they went to sleep by. Then the floor started to sway and a thin drizzle of itchy particles sifted down from nowhere.

Did you know that once five bucks could buy four Classic comics, four quarts of soda and twenty Babe Ruths with enough left over for four packs of cigarettes?

There is yet a small band of radical agriculturists dwelling in the dismal regions who think the NBA is for sissies.

"Gone Fishin'"
Only when chores were done was it time to go fishing, as captured in this painting by folk artist Sandi Wickersham. (Artwork © Sandi Wickersham)

105

BARN DANCES

"The autumnal dances are the best medicine against the threat of winter, isolation again, dangers. The barns were turned into dance halls before the winter hay was cut. The women raised their long skirts and danced toward hell in schottisches, round dances, and square dances. The rafters rang with the music of the old fiddlers and the har-monica players."
    —Meridel LeSueur, "The Ancient People and the Newly Come," 1976

Costume ball

RIGHT: A theatrical barn dance in Calgary, Alberta, brought out an array of costumes for a night of frolicking and merry-making. (Glenbow Archives)

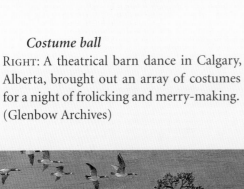

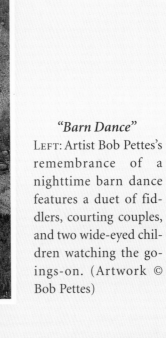

"Barn Dance"

LEFT: Artist Bob Pettes's remembrance of a nighttime barn dance features a duet of fiddlers, courting couples, and two wide-eyed children watching the goings-on. (Artwork © Bob Pettes)

CHAPTER 3

The Future of a Farming Icon

"Barns are counterpoints to rolling land and broad skies. They are focal points in a land of undulating hills and far reaching valleys. Many are truly works of art, each one making a special, artistic statement. Destroy an old barn and the beauty of the countryside is destroyed as well."

—Jerry Apps, *Ethnic History and Beauty of Old Barns*, 1999

To most folk, barns are an integral part of the countryside. When we think back to our rural roots, our mind's vision of the land is ingrained with an image of green rolling hills, far-reaching fields of gold, blue skies dotted by high clouds, and a red barn.

If you hail from the Corn Belt of the Midwest, you may imagine clean, white dairy barns. New Englanders may picture the region's small, red barns. In the Mid-Atlantic, it might be the vast graystone barns. From the West, it's low-slung ranch barns; from the South, it's tobacco barns. In the Pennsylvania Dutch counties, it's an enormous red bank barn with white trim and painted hex signs. In Iowa, it may be a utopian round barn.

The barn is such an essential part of our past that many of us take it for granted. But as agriculture evolves and people move from the farm to the city, the old barn has often fallen derelict, a sad symbol of our changing world. Saving the barn—a true icon of the farm—will be our challenge for the future.

"Fall Plowing"
LEFT: Grant Wood was the quintessential artist of the farmlands. His select palette of colors brought life to his images of the Iowa farms and small towns where he was raised. With a technique of full, rounded dimensions and heavy shading, his trees, haystacks, and plants appeared ripe and bountiful while his depiction of the rolling hills gave the fields all of the glory of the open sea. This painting of a plow at rest before a farm vista was created in 1931. (Deere & Company)

Hayhood perch
INSET: There was no more impressive place to have your picture taken than on the tip-top of the barn hayhood. (Glenbow Archives)

WE HAVE ALL GONE AWAY: THE BARN BUILDER

By Curtis Harnack

Curtis Arthur Harnack was born and bred on the Remsen, Iowa, farm he described in his 1981 memoir *We Have All Gone Away*. From childhood, Harnack sought to be a writer. After graduating from Iowa's Grinnell College, he moved to New York City and Columbia University for a master's degree. He returned to Iowa to teach at Grinnell and subsequently at the University of Iowa's Writer's Workshop.

Whether he was in Iowa or New York, life in Midwestern small towns remained a dominant theme of Harnack's writing. He published a trilogy of novels set in the rural Midwest—*The Work of an Ancient Hand* (1960), *Love and Be Silent* (1962), and *Limits of the Land* (1979)—as well as his memoir of farm life and a sequel, *The Attic* (1993).

In *We Have All Gone Away*, Harnack brings to life the farm smells we all recollect, the sweat and drudgery of the chores we all did, and the simple joys of being a child on a farm that we all can share in remembering.

This excerpt evokes his grandfather and the barn he built on the family farm.

Grandfather built barns during the 1870's in the valley of the Turkey River north of Dubuque. His barns were not squat and heavy-breasted, where the roof line heaves in order to accommodate heaps of grain inside and windows break out in smiles. They rose like stranded ocean vessels out of a sea of prairie grass: solid stone and concrete foundations, neat board-and-batten sides, a canted roof pitched to slough off the heavy snows of Middle-Western winters.

But what's that little house on top? A *cupola*. The strange Latin word was hard for Anglo-Saxon tongues; difficult to imagine Grandfather responsible for this elegantly detailed dream-building—like the image the barn had of itself in grander terms. The cupola of our Lower Barn had scalloped white eaves, tilted side slats like unfurled fans (painted red), and a shell-patterned toy tin roof with a pommel-like steeple—plus a light-ning rod. What's the cupola *for*? I'd ask Uncle Jack, and with a smile and shrug he'd say, "To finish off the barn—just for looks. Pa loved cupolas." It was the only frivolous thing I ever knew about Grandfather.

His sacred carpentry tools, which neatly fitted into compartments of a well-designed handmade box, remained in his close possession until his death in 1931 and now are exhibited in the local county museum. No wonder. They're lifeless implements. These planes, awls, saws, files, drill bits need further explanation. How did they work for a man? None of us can pick them up and proceed. Our flesh feels no connection with this lusterless iron and dry cellular tissue. Something is missing. We're not what our fathers were.

He'd been born in Mecklenburg, Germany, immigrated at age three with his parents to New Orleans, St. Louis, then Iowa, where his father bought a farm. He

Castle

If a man's home is his castle, then a farmer's castle must surely be his or her barn. W. M. Savage was the owner of the world-record-setting racehorse Dan Patch, and built this stately barn as the horse's stable. Complete with onion-dome-topped turrets and heated stalls, Savage's barn was a tribute to his famed horse. What farmer wouldn't wish for the same? The barn crowned Savage's estate in the eponymous town of Savage, Minnesota, before burning down in 1917. (Minnesota Historical Society)

learned carpentry when a young man in order to accumulate a stake to go west with the railroad, which had received land (two miles on either side) from the government as incentive to lay tracks to Sioux City, linking that outpost on the Missouri River to Chicago six hundred miles east. Paying eight dollars an acre in gold, he claimed one hundred and sixty acres and immediately began erecting barns—the house could come later. He reserved nine acres for outbuildings, yards, orchards, groves—nine extravagant acres that would never yield crops, never "pay." All his work with cut lumber made him hungry for trees, of which there were none, and from eastern Iowa's wooded coulees he transplanted seedlings of walnut, oak, cedar, birch, maple, pine, as well as fruit trees and shrubs which have flowered each spring for the last hundred years. This barn builder had an affinity for the immortal aspects of wood, knew that Jesus, dying for the sins of the world, ensuring life-everlasting for those who believed, had done it on a cross of wood. . . .

Grandfather's heart was pure and terrible. He was the stern German father of legend who hushed the children and made them work, who loved them so strongly he beat them when they were the slightest bit wicked, and who never touched a drop of liquor but kept rye whiskey in the kitchen cabinet, liniment for his achy legs, scoffing at the lushes of the neighborhood who were outraged, who'd probably, Grandfather felt, gladly lick his legs if given half a chance. Laziness, softness, and mischievousness were to be purged from children, and the sooner they learned the hard lessons of life the better. Every year in fall after corn picking his six children (a seventh died at birth) filled mattress ticks with fresh cornhusks. But little Jack complained, said why empty out the old only to put in more cornhusks, to which Grandfather replied, "You'll find out." By January the old shucks in Jack's ticking were so shredded he had nothing but lumps left, he was miserable. And Grandpa smiled.

From 1895 to 1925, those leaping years for Ameri-

Wild West barn

Most western ranch barns were built for storing hay for beef cattle instead of housing dairy cows. This venerable barn in the foothills of the Teton Mountains, Teton National Park, Wyoming, is made up of a central stall with two outer sheds built onto it. The gable roof has a broken pitch, sloping more gently over the additions. (Photograph © Dennis Frates)

can agriculture, his land value increased to six hundred dollars an acre and he made money on crops and herds. Only once, in the Depression of 1907, were times so tough that the family ate hand-ground cornmeal mush laced with fresh milk. Uncle Jack and my aunts, who told of the hardship, couldn't bear to have the porridge served, though we seven grandchildren insisted on tasting *at least once* this galling substance—found it delicious. Grandpa owed nobody money, never bought what he couldn't pay cash for, and so, in the midst of the 1930's Depression, there was nothing for us to fear, not even fear itself; we could eat off the land, burn wood from our huge grove, make-do with hand-me-down clothes from the attic, for nothing had ever been thrown away (on a farm there's no place to throw it), not even Grandmother's high-button shoes.

I was four when Grandfather died, and I remember him only as he looked in the dull-penny coffin, earth-still behind the lace scrim which fell from the open lid: the first dead person I'd seen, since my father, who'd succumbed three years earlier, I'd not yet heard of or even missed. No doubt I was allowed to view the corpse because the funeral proceedings were so genial. Heavy scent of funeral flowers, self-congratulatory heartiness. Grandfather, this grand octogenarian, sculpturally smooth in his repose, was actually in heaven; about such a good man there couldn't be the slightest doubt. Hoards of relatives filled Grandfather's retirement house, which he'd designed and built by hand with the aid of his two sons (my father and Uncle Jack), who married two sisters and had taken over the homestead. After such a successful life, what was there to be sad about? Grandfather moved out and away from us on an island of honor, the way Elijah was assumpted into the skies. Everything he'd created here on earth was going to live on. . . .

When the barns were finished, house construction got underway, my grandparents meanwhile living in a shack six feet wide and ten feet long called by us "the little granary," for sacks of chicken feed were sometimes kept there. Mostly it was an abandoned junk shed where hens laid eggs in impossible places, under the hand corn sheller or in a dismembered chick brooder. Such a tiny cabin, with only two windows, was a strange shelter for the beginnings of our dynasty. My ancient grandmother, who peeped at us through thick octagonal glasses, from an immense distance, spoke in a squeaky nineteenth-century voice of no resonance, and when she passed ninety, hunched over more and more into a

Autumn
ABOVE: Surrounded by fall colors, an abandoned log barn rests in the South Carolina mountains. (Photograph © Robert Clark)

Weathered barn
FACING PAGE: Starched by the sun's rays, the wallboards of this ancient gambrel-roof Illinois barn have faded to the same golden-gray color as the surrounding autumn grasses. (Photograph © Willard Clay)

little buttonhook—yet she'd once been tall and strong enough to labor like a man in the fields, working oxen on the family farm near the Mississippi. She recalled how her brother loped across the sod one day, frantic with the news President Lincoln had been shot. She flung down her hoe and hurried to the house, though the news was five days old, the caravan to Springfield beginning. The last time she reminisced about it, sitting on an upended orange crate near the back stoop of her house, a bottle of Pepsi-Cola in her hand, Roosevelt had just died.

And yet, with these upheavals and passings of generations, Grandfather's solid barns remained, always bearing some intimate relation to the earth.

Amish Barn Raising

"I don't make blueprints. Oh, sure, I make drawings sometimes. To figure the beam lengths. But how it goes up? I know all that."
— Master Amish barn builder Josie Miller, quoted in Randy Leffingwell's *The American Barn*, 1997

Built the old-fashioned way
In Amish farming communities, barns are still built the old-fashioned way: Friends and neighbors gather together to erect the edifice—often in one day's time. Workers arrived bright and early at this Lancaster County, Pennsylvania, barn raising to get a jump on the day. (Photograph © Jerry Irwin)

Finishing touches
By evening, the walls and roof were assembled on the prelaid foundation and the roof was covered at this Amish barn raising in Ohio. All that was left to do was paint the barn, work that was saved for another day. (Photograph © Jerry Irwin)

Raising the roof
Some 100 volunteer carpenters swarmed over the roof beams as this Lancaster County, Pennsylvania, barn took shape. (Photograph © Jerry Irwin)

Farewell, the Barns

By Patricia Penton Leimbach

Patricia Penton Leimbach is farming's Erma Bombeck. Like Bombeck, she is a sage philosopher on the trials and tribulations of everyday life. She writes with a sharp pen about the joys and troubles, the hard work and humor, the meaning and value of rural living.

Leimbach was raised on a fruit farm near Lorain, Ohio. Alongside her husband Paul, a fourth-generation farmer, she has run End o'Way farm in Vermilion, Ohio, for more than four decades.

It is through her writing that Leimbach has become one of the best-known farm women in North America. For many years, she authored the weekly "Country Wife" column in the Elyria, Ohio, *Chronicle Telegram* newspaper. She also has three books to her credit, *A Thread of Blue Denim* (1974), *All My Meadows* (1977), and *Harvest of Bittersweet* (1987), all of which are filled with wit and wisdom culled from her firsthand knowledge of everything from raising puppies to driving farm tractors.

In this essay, she reminisces on the loss of the family's barn and the special place in her heart that barns of have held.

The big barn is gone. A bulldozer came Monday, pushed its shattered foundation down the barnyard slope and covered it with topsoil, as the waves close over a shipwreck. Only empty space there and the memories of children. . . .

People don't talk much of the work hours that pass in a barn, of the great loads of hay rushed in ahead of a summer shower, the boosting and stacking of bales. These things are mentioned only facetiously to illustrate how hard we slaved as children. No, it's the fun we dote upon, the forbidden pleasures indulged beyond the disapproving eyes of grownups.

How many times did my husband Paul come storming into my kitchen after morning chores muttering about the way the darned kids—sons, cousins, neighbors—had booby-trapped the haymow rearranging the bales. To the children they were tunnels, forts, playhouses, but to the farmer discharging his chores they were a menace. I let him rave on the pretext that the barn was beyond my jurisdiction. What I knew from long memory was that fun in the hay barn was more vital to posterity than the orderly dispatch of hay and straw to cattle.

In my childhood we ran like monkeys about the beams of our barn playing tag and hide-n-seek, swinging Tarzan-like from one mow to the other on a rope hung from the roof beam. I remember once falling from the haymow to the ground floor of our neighbor's barn, lying there unable to breathe. It wasn't something I went home and confessed to my parents. No more did we confess, my brothers and I, that we'd been smoking corn silk in that same barn. Somehow they learned, and we got the strapping of our lives.

Strange and wonderful stuff made its way to the upper loft of the big barn—egg crates, corn shellers, seed cleaners, hand plows and horse cultivators, barrels, shutters, sleighs, an old toilet stool and sink, wire baskets, spare doors and windows, broken chairs, and tools beyond memory. How intriguing it was to pore over this junk, rearrange, and work it into the stuff of make-believe.

This barn is not the first that we've dismantled. You buy your neighbor's farm, you own another old barn that will forever carry his name. Our neighbor Pete Newberry's hip-roofed barn had a grace about it that

A barn full of memories
A visit to the old haymow brings a remembrance of times past on the Kluenker farm in Manitowoc, Wisconsin. (Photograph © Richard Hamilton Smith)

Barn fire
Flames engulf a gambrel-roof barn and its duet of silos on a farm in Chisago County, Minnesota, in the 1940s. (Minnesota Historical Society)

our big barn lacked, but the roof was already beyond repair when we acquired it. Pete wanted to re-roof it once, but Paul's grandfather, who was no great shakes at repairing things, talked him out of it, to our everlasting grief. It had to go. We needed machinery storage an old cattle barn couldn't provide.

The fellow who bargained for the removal of its silvery-grey siding never came back to pay us. I suppose that somewhere it contributed to a bogus reproduction, a mockery of America's vanished grandeur. There's something profane about a cocktail lounge done out in barn siding. A weathered board, like a weathered farmer, deserves better things.

The skeleton of that old hip-roofed barn, raped of its lovely siding, stood there naked against the sky for several years before Paul pulled it down, the huge proud beams hewn of virgin timber, oak and chestnut, the ladders mounting to the peak—a Mondrian drawing on a blue canvas.

I often wondered, as I admired it, what stories it could tell beyond the round of morning and evening chores. Pete Newberry's wife was my father-in-law's cousin, so in a way our farm lore was intertwined. Pete's sister-in-law, the last of her generation, spoke of the glorious day in 1920 when the neighbors all came for the barn raising: "I tell you, that was quite a barn in its day. We sat on the front porch and watched the men raise those big timbers. It was just amazing with what ease they did it. I remember that we made ham sandwiches and there was a keg of beer."

Would the old barn speak of the pride it gave a man to have a barn so fine, of the hope it instilled for the future? Would it tell of a hired girl seduced in the haymow, of the hired man who hid whiskey bottles in the granary? Would it come forth with the basic truth

whispered by the neighbors through the years that this was too extravagant a structure for a struggling farmer in the 1920s and that it contributed sadly to his defeat?

Demolishing these old barns and disposing of the accumulated mass is no small task. A farmer can be forgiven at that point for longing for a barn fire. Unfortunately, barns don't burn on demand. A barn's burning is a tragic fact farmers live with. You hear it in rural conversation: ". . . the year the barn burned." I can tick them off in my head, all the people who lost barns.

We lost ours when I was still a child. It seemed like the end of the world, coming as it did the same year our father died. I remember the scene of dejection in our kitchen that night. Mayor Cooper drove his black Packard out from town, sat on a too-small chair holding his hat against his ample stomach, and apologized that the fire department hadn't been able to do much.

The day neighbor Schmalz's barn burned Paul and Orrin saw the smoke from the field where they were planting potatoes. They unhooked the planter and raced down with two tractors thinking there would be machinery to tow. Bev Schmalz had dialed 911 and run waving a red bandanna to summon her husband and brother-in-law from their corn planting.

The tire trucks glided in behind the drying shed, their sirens tapering off as Paul hooked his tractor to a lime spreader and pulled it to safety. They unwrapped their hoses and began dousing the scorched grain silos to the relief of the neighbors who were by then all there, the same crowd that share our picnics, weddings, graduations, funerals.

A barn burning rates right up there with a farm sale or a church social for attracting a crowd. On that warm Saturday morning people converged from four

"Barns at Glen Gardner"
Artist Wanda Gág grew up in Minnesota farm country, and this 1943 lithograph captures the feel of hand-cut boards and fieldstone that make up an old barn. Gág is best known for her 1928 masterpiece children's book *Millions of Cats*, which won the prestigious Newberry Honor Award. (Minnesota Historical Society)

Slouching toward earth
The last step in the fall of a barn is often a precipitous lean toward the earth from which its materials came. Like a farmyard version of the Leaning Tower of Pisa, this veteran barn in the Berkshire Mountains of Massachusetts tilted precariously with the helping hand of gravity. (Photograph © Ian Adams)

townships, each relieved that the smoke was not anchored in his piece of real estate, looking on then with morbid fascination.

The Schmalz brothers leaned against their machine shop and watched helplessly. It wasn't a cattle barn, so there were no animals in peril, but they had lost a back hoe and a brand new fertilizer spreader. "Never been used," said Russell glumly. Only the previous day they'd taken delivery on $16,000 worth of chemicals. With grain prices at a ten-year low they didn't need this.

That barn had its own story to tell. It was, perhaps, the oldest barn in the area but had weathered well because it had a slate roof and owners who were fastidious with building repairs. On a sad Depression morning long ago the previous owner hanged himself from one of the barn beams. To my children, Schmalz's barn was the convenient hangout for the neighborhood gang. It stood just uphill from our one-room schoolhouse at the juncture of two township roads. There they had played cops-n-robbers, kick-the-can, and basketball. I remember especially the autumn of the great tomato wars scheduled for Schmalz's barn in late September when the fruit was ripe and juicy. There they languished in the diminishing light of summer evenings shooting the breeze, planning great futures.

The township trustees hung about often on the oval in front of the barn to plot the day's activities, waiting for a tank of oil or a load of slag. (One or another of the Schmalz brothers was usually on the township board.) Many people valued that barn for the associations it had to precious people and happy times, to a life that recedes with every death and each passing landmark.

This barn that died today appeared on the tax duplicate in 1849. Our family took possession in 1875, and six generations of Leimbach children have known and enjoyed it. I avoided the scene all summer as Orrin worked at the dismantling, sorting, moving. Too much of my life was invested there.

What startles and alarms me is how rapidly all was effaced once that bulldozer set to work. Who will ever know there was a playhouse of enchantment there "when like our sires, our sons are gone?"

Farewell
The last light of day reflects off the faded wooden walls of an old barn in Bureau County, Illinois. (Photograph © Joseph Kayne)

Barn Door Hoods

tulip

swastika

for bird's nest

Pennsylvania

Barn Doors

glassless "transom light" and a King size door-prop to last the winter.

Barn door Roller

1840

Pennsylvania
c. 1750

Door in a door

Sheathed Dutch door

Original shutter

Glass added
c. 1840

Connecticut
c. 1820

Pre-roller
Double-runner sliding door.

New Hampshire

mid 1700s

I Remember Barns

By Eric Sloane

"I am sad that tomorrow's youth will never know a simple harvest, see a haystack, hear a steam locomotive whistle, sleep in a hay barn or fish in a quiet stream. But, I'm thankful for having known it and glad I can recollect bits and pass it on." So said Eric Sloane of the impetus behind his famous paintings, drawings, and books chronicling America and American folklore.

Born Everard Jean Hindrichs in New York City in 1905, he ran away from home when he was sixteen. He supported himself with his skill as a budding artist by painting lettering on barns, post boxes, or store signs in exchange for room and board. Lettering names and numbers on early airplanes led him to discover clouds and meteorology, and he subsequently became America's first TV weatherman. His interest in weather also inspired a fascination with farming, leading to his great love affair with the beginnings of America. He adopted the name Eric Sloane made from the four central letters of "America" and in tribute to his painting teacher John Sloan.

Sloane's fame rests on the thirty-eight books he published, many of them on American folklore, including his most famous work, *An Age of Barns* (1967), a study of the barn and its history. Among his other accomplishments was the inspiration for the national revival of the ringing of church bells on the Fourth of July in a Congressional Act of 1963.

This short essay on barns comes from his book *I Remember America* (1971).

I remember barns because, as a painter of them, that is exactly what I have *had* to do; I do not paint on location. It has always seemed to me that the best way to capture the mood of any scene is to regard it as an echo in the mind, after I have made photographs or sketches. Such a recollection at the easel is that much less photographic, more a memory and therefore more a free design.

My peculiar reputation of being "America's barn painter" has often resulted in amusing confusion. There are still those who think this title refers to some sort of house painter, and seldom does a month go by without someone whose barn needs a coat of paint requesting an estimate from "Sloane, the barn painter."

Although I regard nostalgia as a dread disease, still it is difficult to paint scenes of long ago without some reverence being evoked. Americans have been the last to find any merit whatsoever in obsolescence and even less in decay, so my audience is usually quick to be critical. One gallery asked if I would do a painting of a "better-kept barn" for a client who owned a prosperous farm and could not bear to see any farm buildings in disrepair. I also recall one buyer who brought a painting back to me, asking me to restore some of the missing boards and broken windows and to trim the overgrown grass. After all, he argued, it was exactly what I'd done to my own old barn.

I feel that when Nature is allowed to have her way in reducing buildings to a state of "pleasing decay," the effect can reach a rare height of artistic fascination. This is, however, a complex matter because not all ruin is pleasing. Life too mirrors Nature. Man's life passes away all too quickly, and even the best memory is, in some way, a ruin.

"Barn Doors"
A sampling of vintage barn doors and hoods from Eric Sloane's 1967 masterpiece of barn history and folklore, *An Age of Barns*. (Artwork © the Estate of Eric Sloane)

> *"On a windy day in April, standing inside an old barn is like standing in the midst of a great orchestra. As the wind blows around the corners and shakes the side walls, the barn talks back in squeaks and creaks and moans. In the huge expanse of the open barn, the sounds echo back and forth, creating an audio beauty that few have heard."*
>
> —Jerry Apps, *Ethnic History and Beauty of Old Barns*, 1999

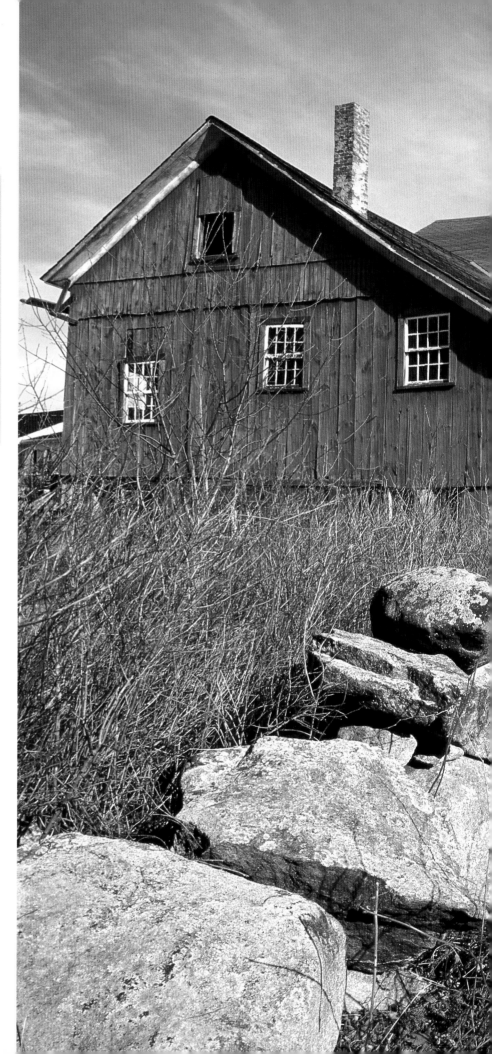

Working barn
A wall made of fieldstone leads the way up to a gable-roof barn and its cross-gable addition in Royalston, Massachusetts. (Photograph © Paul Rezendes)

Barn beauty
Details of worn barn wood and a rusted galvanized-steel roof display the beauty of a barn. (Photograph © Richard Hamilton Smith)

There is no building that does not develop some unexpected charm with age; but the early American barn, taking into consideration its reasons for being, I've found to be an exceptional and impressive subject. The growth of moss, the dust of old hay, the powdering of mortar in joints, the mellowing of cut stone, the aging of wood—all things usually thought to be unfortunate—are really Nature's triumph and worth regarding with some (at least artistic) respect. When eyes are opened to pleasing decay, it is sometimes difficult to focus on anything else. Ancient homes have a way of adapting to the changing times; with new curtains and a coat of paint, the appealing quality of age vanishes all too soon, but an old barn has an aura of persistence, stubbornly shrouded in the mood of its own time.

Old farm buildings are monuments to a dead and vanished America. The United States was founded on agrarianism, and the farm was the living symbol of our economy, but that national philosophy has now become obsolete. Replaced by capitalism, the old-time farmer is vanished Americana along with the agrarian credo.

Nonetheless, its truth and logic, its reverence for the earth and the God who created it, make it an everlasting religion. Perhaps after capitalism has expended itself (as some logicians predict), man may spend his last efforts on earth in an attempt to return to agrarianism.

After having painted hundreds of pictures of barns and having sketched details of thousands, I have sometimes looked back and wondered if I could have been mistaken to do so. I so passionately believe in the merits of agrarianism that I could have been carried away by nostalgic emotion. Perhaps the magic of my subject had only been an illusion? Yet the incense of hay and animal odors do seem to linger even after a century or two; the sense of harbor from the outside world given by an old barn does prevail like a persistent ghost. To me a barn's age has actual dimension and proportion; even after it has fallen and its timbers disappeared, there seems to be some part of it lingering, looming above the stone foundations. All this may sound absurd: I am simply stating what I feel.

Cajun barn
A Cajun barn in Saint Francisville, Louisiana, with the typical large, open front entrance, side corncribs, and overhead hayloft. The gambrel roof is crowned by a raised monitor, allowing better ventilation for the haymow. (Photograph © Ian Adams)

Historically speaking, barns have usually been overlooked, although they speak more truthfully of the past than most architectural monuments. Their sameness of construction in America is often regarded as a lack of originality, or perhaps an indication of the early Puritan starvation of self-expression. Actually their sameness represents nothing other than a reverence for tradition. The farmer of the past had much more building education and appreciation of art than today's farmer, yet there was no urge for self-expression or for "change for the sake of change." From Maine to Virginia (though nationalities and personalities differed), you will find beams cut in the very same manner and fastened together into designs almost as if they had all been done by the same person.

In the study of barn architecture, you come closer to pure Americana than in old homes in which European and English influences all but eliminated any standard American style. Both in research that proved useful and for pure personal pleasure, I think I've done well to have remembered barns.

Hauling manure
A farmer hauls stale straw and manure from his cross-gable barn in 1910 while his workhorse waits patiently. (Minnesota Historical Society)

BARN SMELLS

"I'm glad the farm smells haven't changed. I'd forgotten them just a little but only to the extent that I'd ceased to recall them. They were there all the time. Thirty-five years or a thousand, hay in the barn smells just the same and so do cows and little calves and burning leaves in November. . . . There's the horsey smell that makes a man smell like a man—substantial and trustworthy—and the rich aroma of the barnyard that recalls the bounty of the earth and the opulent crops that are sure to come another year when it rains a little more. . . . Lots of you little farm boys think you'd like to live in the city when you grow up. You honestly think that, but you really wouldn't like it. So many farm boys never come to like the city, even after they've lived there fifty years. There is always something they want and can't get—a little itch they can't scratch. You can never quite figure out what it is they miss. It's the smells."

—Romeyn Berry, *Dirt Roads to Stoneposts*, 1949

"City folk think of barns, especially if they are large and red (the barns, not the city folk), as wonderful, picturesque, rustic, quintessential, evocative, almost spiritual places. Until they actually get inside one and smell it."

—Terry Chamberlain, *The ABC's of Farming*, 1999

"The barn should be located far enough from the house to prevent the aromas of the stables and kitchen from mingling."

—Isaac Phillips Roberts, *The Farmstead: The Making of the Rural Home and the Lay-Out of the Farm*, 1900

Winter clouds over red barns
A string of small connected barns weathers the winter in Hartford, Vermont. (Photograph © Paul Rezendes)

Barn Again

By Barbara Pahl

Historic barns were considered doomed when the U.S. National Trust for Historic Preservation and *Successful Farming* magazine launched the revolutionary Barn Again! program in 1987. Obsolete for modern farming needs

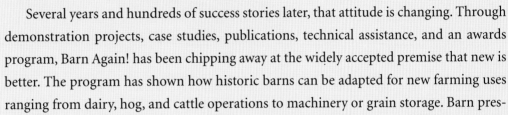

and too expensive to maintain as family heirlooms, old barns appeared destined to be preserved only in photographs and memories.

Several years and hundreds of success stories later, that attitude is changing. Through demonstration projects, case studies, publications, technical assistance, and an awards program, Barn Again! has been chipping away at the widely accepted premise that new is better. The program has shown how historic barns can be adapted for new farming uses ranging from dairy, hog, and cattle operations to machinery or grain storage. Barn preservation techniques have proven to be cost-effective alternatives to tearing down the old barn and putting up a new building.

Barbara Pahl is the director of the U.S. National Trust for Historic Preservation's Mountains/Plains office in Denver, Colorado, which oversees the Barn Again! program.

Situated between *barmitzvah* and *barnacle* in Webster's Dictionary you can find the word *barn*. A barn is defined as a large structure used to store grain or house livestock. The word barn was derived from the English *bern*: *ern* was the word for barley, with *aern* meaning place or house. Far more than a mere storehouse for grain or animals, barns have become powerful symbols representing a swiftly fading epoch in American history.

During the twentieth century America was transformed from a primarily rural, agrarian society to an industrial, urban society. By mid century, America's urban scene was changing so rapidly that many people began to be concerned with preserving pieces of the past for future generations. By the 1960s, there was a growing national historic preservation movement in the United States and many treasures of the urban landscape were saved from the wrecking ball.

A very different situation existed out in the countryside, however. The family farm was in decline and with it the magnificent monoliths of the plains and prairies, the American barns. No longer the vital center of the farm, barns were victims of progress, made obsolete by modern agricultural practices. Relegated to storage and occasional use, these proud structures began to decay and disappear. Because the barn has been such a recognizable feature of the American landscape, many people became alarmed with the rapidity of its decline.

Farmers and ranchers have played important roles in American history. The structures that they developed, built, and used are just as significant as the museums, theaters, and cathedrals of the urban centers. Barns are not located on busy streets with thousands of people walking by each day. Barns are often far off the beaten path, and may be seen only by a privileged

Barn Again!
The logo of the Barn Again! program, launched by the U.S. National Trust for Historic Preservation and *Successful Farming* magazine.

Utopian ideals live on
A red round barn shines against a dark sky in Irasburg, Vermont. (Photograph © Jerry Irwin)

few. But their absence would leave a gaping hole in the fabric of America's built environment.

In 1987, the National Trust for Historic Preservation in partnership with *Successful Farming* magazine set out to reverse this trend and rescue America's barns. The result of this timely partnership was the Barn Again! program, a national program designed to help America's rural historic property owners save their barns. The program brought together architects, engineers, and construction experts, as well as agricultural experts, who determined that far from being useless relics, historic barns could once again become the focal point of America's farms and ranches. Demonstration projects were undertaken to modify historic barns for modern agricultural purposes.

Since the program was founded, thousands of farmers, ranchers, small towns, and rural preservation organizations have contacted the National Trust. Hundreds of barns have been rescued from oblivion. By providing information about the value of historic preservation and by demonstrating that preservation and practicality are not mutually exclusive, the Barn Again! program has been able to bring about a minor revolution in the way rural property owners view their historic buildings.

Annual Barn Again! awards recognize farm families for their contributions to the preservation of our nation's agricultural heritage. Awards draw national attention to the personal efforts of farmers and ranchers who are quietly doing their part to preserve historic rural resources. Award-winning projects are used as models to demonstrate preservation techniques and new uses for older barns. From 1988 to 2000, Barn Again! honored 154 farmers and ranchers from Maine to Oregon for making heritage a part of daily life on the farm.

Barn Again!'s most recent award winners exemplify the spirit and practical message of the program. Indiana's Joey and Sid Kubesch, along with Joey's mother, Alice Cole, won the 2001 Farm Heritage Award by saving four separate barns on two farms originally purchased by James O. Cole over 100 years ago. James O. Cole was grandfather to none other than song writer

Cole Porter, the composer of such standards as "Night and Day" and "It's De-Lovely," and, perhaps not surprisingly, a tune entitled "Farming." Porter used one of the farms as his home base during visits back to Indiana. Memorabilia from his career can currently be found in the 1916 brick farm house where Alice Cole lives today.

The Kubesches have preserved an important piece of Indiana history while maintaining useful facilities for their farming operation. The Kubesches do not consider themselves preservationists in the strictest sense, but they have a preservationist respect and appreciation for the past. "We are keenly aware of the importance and significance of history," Joey says.

All four barns are constructed of native timber and secured with wooden pegs. They feature handcrafted woodwork and custom-made gate hinges and latches dating from the 1930s. And they have been carefully maintained through the years. "Keeping the buildings in regular use has been the best means of preserving them," Joey says. "Preservation is ongoing. We replace materials only when needed, but we do it with appropriate materials." That means a coat of paint every ten years or so, periodic repairs to roofs, sliding doors, and windows, and in some cases, installing steel rods in the haymows to keep the barns straight. The Kubesches have spent $50,000 on their four barns since 1974. With an estimated replacement value of $320,000 for the four buildings, the economics are obvious, though "figuring replacement versus repair was never really an issue," Joey adds.

Joey's grandfather Omar Cole, cousin to Cole Porter, started a family tradition of raising Angus cattle, exhibiting the Grand Champion Angus heifer at the International Livestock Exposition of 1938. When Joey and Sid returned to run the farms in 1970, they revived the registered purebred Angus herd that Omar had started. They now run about 220 head on 850 acres, along with soybeans, hay, wheat, corn, and timber in the shadows of their barns—and of their history.

Farmers, ranchers and other owners of historic barns have come to count on the Barn Again! program to provide timely and personal assistance in solving

BARN AGAIN! CONTACT INFORMATION

Barn Again! staff members conduct workshops and training in barn rehabilitation for farmers, ranchers, agricultural professionals, and public and private sector preservation professionals, and advise local and state agencies on developing their own programs to promote and encourage rehabilitation of historic barns. Barn Again! also offers publications and other educational materials with technical information about barn rehabilitation and model projects completed by farmers and ranchers. *Successful Farming* magazine has published more than twenty-five articles demonstrating that preserving historic barns is good farming practice.

The program has distributed 15,000 copies of *Barn Again! A Guide to Rehabilitation of Older Farm Buildings*. Barn Again! has also cosponsored an exhibit on historic barns with the National Building Museum in Washington, D. C., and an hour-long documentary for public television with Nebraska Educational Television. Barn Again! has initiated a series of technical bulletins providing in-depth information about particular barn rehabilitation problems. Titles currently available in the *Barn Aid* Series include: *Barn Aid #1: Barn Foundations, Barn Aid #2: New Spaces for Old Places, Barn Aid #3: Barn Exteriors and Painting*, and *Barn Aid #4: Barn Roofs*.

You may contact Barn Again! at (303) 623-1504 or visit the website at www.barnagain.org.

barn rehabilitation problems. The Barn Again! staff answers technical questions and provides advice on adapting historic barns for new farming uses, listing properties in the National Register of Historic Places, and applying for federal tax credits. Barn Again! is nationally recognized as the clearinghouse for information about preserving historic barns. Our resources are used by preservationists, architects, contractors, agricultural professionals, and the media, as well as owners of historic barns. More than 1,100 farmers received Barn Again! assistance in 2000. In fourteen years the program has directly assisted 8,000 barn owners in all fifty states and several foreign countries.

Bank barn
A bank barn is reflected in the waters of a farm pond in Logan County, Ohio. (Photograph © Ian Adams)

This old barn
Frost and snow cover a majestic old barn in Ross County, Ohio. (Photograph © Ian Adams)

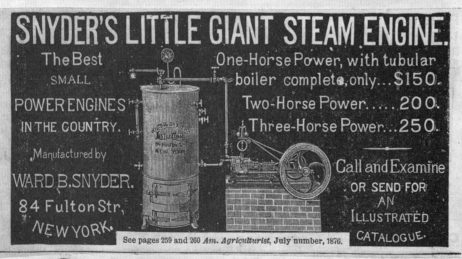

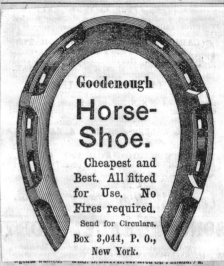